MW00353649

RAWHIDE

A HISTORY OF TELEVISION'S LONGEST CATTLE DRIVE

by **DAVID R. GREENLAND**

Dedicated to

Wilbert Dinges,

who spent his life on the land.

RAWHIDE
A HISTORY OF TELEVISION'S LONGEST CATTLE DRIVE
©2011 DAVID R. GREENLAND

ALL RIGHTS RESERVED.

All rights reserved. No part of this book may be reproduced or distributed, in print, recorded, live or digital form, without express written permission of the copyright holder. However, excerpts of up to 500 words may be reproduced online if they include the following information, "This is an excerpt from Rawhide by David R. Greenland."

Published in the USA by:

BEARMANOR MEDIA
P.O. BOX 71426
ALBANY, GEORGIA 31708
www.BearManorMedia.com

ISBN-10: 1-59393-863-2

ISBN-13: 978-1-59393-863-5

DESIGN AND LAYOUT: VALERIE THOMPSON

TABLE OF CONTENTS

ACKNOWLEDGMENTS

While working on another book nearly twenty years ago, I learned that the actors who worked primarily as guest stars in television often have memories that are understandably hazy. The late Claude Akins summed up the problem quite succinctly: "I did so many different shows back then that asking me to remember a particular episode of something is like asking what I had for dinner Tuesday night three weeks ago. I have no idea."

Similarly, I once ran into the late Alan Hale, Jr. (best known as the Skipper on *Gilligan's Island*) at Chicago's O'Hare Airport, and when I mentioned an episode of *Bonanza* he appeared in, he proceeded to describe an episode of *Gunsmoke* he had done. I did not have the heart to tell him he was confused.

Some of the retired thespians I contacted for this book had no specific recollections of their *Rawhide* experiences, even after viewing a videotape of their performance. One gentleman chuckled and said, "I was on *Rawhide*? Really?" On the other hand, a few were very helpful, with the exception of one who will remain nameless. After growling, "I don't remember a damn thing," he hinted that he might be persuaded to come up with "one or two" anecdotes in exchange for "some bucks." I politely passed.

Those actors who were helpful, or were at least willing to help, include the late Charles Gray, Gregory Walcott, Jan Shepard, Morgan Woodward, L.Q. Jones, Gregg Palmer, Warren Stevens, Tom Reese, the late Richard Devon, and director Ted Post. Thanks to Dan Turpin, who put me in touch with a few of these people and others.

The majority of the photographs distributed to various media outlets for publicity purposes by the CBS Television Network were obtained from private collectors or memorabilia dealers. No copyright ownership by the author is claimed or implied. Special thanks to Milton T. Moore and Jerry Ohlinger for help with many of these illustrations.

All 217 episodes of *Rawhide*, including the unaired version of the pilot, were collected and viewed for this book, a process that literally took years and could not have been completed without the assistance of Barbara Douglass, Claude Faulkner, Boyd Magers, Lanny Tucker and Gary Yoggy.

And a very special thanks to my oldest friend, Barry Craig, for helping me locate and explore most of *Rawhide*'s shooting sites while I lived in Los Angeles and on subsequent visits.

Finally, I greatly appreciated the advice, encouragement, and various forms of support from my family, friends and various acquaintances, particularly Doug Cameron, Harriet Carlson, Bruce Dinges, Chris Gill, Paul Greenland, Jim Guarino, Steve Homan, Jeff Kadet, Boyd Magers, James Rosin, Lanny Tucker, and especially my wife, Cleo.

Skillfully working their magic as this book moved through the production process were production manager Sandy Grabman, editor Annette Lloyd, publisher Ben Ohmart, and book designer-typesetter Valerie Thompson.

DAVID R. GREENLAND
AUGUST 2010

FOREWORD
BY CHARLES GRAY

AUTHOR'S NOTE: Between September 2007 and April 2008, actor Charles Gray and I exchanged four letters and had one brief telephone conversation. I sent him several of his appearances on *Rawhide* as well as other shows, and he agreed to write a foreword for this book. Regrettably, as I was preparing to mail him specific episodes he requested, I learned he had passed away August 2, 2008. In looking over our correspondence I realized Mr. Gray had provided me with a sufficient number of comments and recollections that may very well have been included in his intended contribution. With very minor editing, I present the thoughts of Charles "Clay Forrester" Gray.

DAVID:

First let me thank you for the kindness and generosity you have shown by sending me those two old tapes from times of youth and vigor! I do remember being on a couple of episodes before officially joining the cast, but I'm afraid seeing them didn't bring back any significant memories.

I want to commend you on behalf of all "old timers" for your active interest in and dedication to the Western genre, of which I am fond since this will always be part of our common growth and heritage. Bravo! Keep it up!

Thanks for sending along that one episode of *Bonanza* I did. I enjoyed working with that company of actors, but I couldn't remember the title—one of my senior moments.

Yes, I would love to have the *Alias Smith & Jones* episode, since I fell in love with Vera Miles. One helluva lady!

Charles Gray. Photo courtesy of Boyd Magers.

Of course I would be interested in more *Rawhides*. You say you have them all? I have to tell you that as much as I enjoyed seeing the one I had a hand in writing, it also reminded me of why I decided to leave the show—I wrote it for the Clay Forrester character but the producer gave it to Eric Fleming instead! A sore spot, to be sure.

No, I don't recall which episode was my last, but I'm sure you will figure that out eventually. You no doubt know that we didn't always make the shows in the order they were broadcast, explaining why Clay appeared to be joining the drive the week after he was already shown being there. As you suggest, the network more than likely wanted to show the Christmas episode during the holiday week.

Nor can I help you determine why an episode I did in 1962 wasn't shown until 1964. Could it have been a repeat? Yes, I was long gone by 1964 regardless of what the historians say!

I can't say I really got to know any of the other cast members very well, although I did enjoy their company. Such is the nature of film work. I knew I was being substituted for Sheb Wooley, and there might have been some momentary thought given to my stepping into Fleming's boots if he followed through on his occasional threats to quit. I can't say for sure at this late date.

I may not be your best choice for writing a foreword, but this is not a refusal. I am honored to be considered and will give it a good try. I will also send you a shot of Clay under separate cover soon.

I am open any time to another phone conversation, though around noon finds me near food and relaxation. If I can be of any help with whatever, do not hesitate to say so.

I hope this finds you well and immersed in your project—you handle words very well. My fond wishes go with you in all this and hope you understand my tardiness. Good luck to you in your writing endeavors.

Sincere & warm regards,
CHARLES GRAY

PREFACE

Every generation has its fictional folk heroes, popular icons who stimulate the imagination and represent a positive view of life. For Baby Boomers, especially those born before the mid-1950s, many of those heroes were cowboys and Old West lawmen who dominated the television schedule from 1949, when Hopalong Cassidy and the Lone Ranger made their home screen debuts, to roughly the mid-1960s. The truly golden age of the television Western started with the 1955 premieres of *The Life and Legend of Wyatt Earp*, *Cheyenne*, and the classic *Gunsmoke*. By 1958 there were more than thirty Westerns on the air, a phenomenon to which *Time* magazine devoted a cover story ("The American Morality Play") in its March 30, 1959 issue.

Hollywood, being no less commercially minded then as it is today, cashed in on the huge popularity of these programs by licensing a wide array of cowboy merchandise. Collectively, my two brothers and I eventually owned a Davy Crockett coonskin cap, Roy Rogers hats, Roy Rogers raincoat, Hopalong Cassidy wristwatch, *Gunsmoke* and *Have Gun Will Travel* guns and holsters, Wyatt Earp badge and vest, Dodge City and Fort Apache play sets, Johnny Yuma (*The Rebel*) cap, *Maverick* derringer, *Lone Ranger* mask and handcuffs, *Bonanza* Viewmaster reels, several TV cowboys and horses (including *Rawhide*'s Gil Favor) manufactured by Hartland Plastics, hardcover books of *The Rifleman* and *Tales of Wells Fargo* published by Whitman, dozens of comic books, and a *Rawhide* canteen. Older Western enthusiasts who grew up watching B movies at Saturday afternoon matinees had such colorful idols as Sunset Carson and Lash LaRue; younger fans had Cheyenne Bodie and Rowdy Yates, to name only two of literally dozens.

In the late 1950s and early 1960s my hometown did not have a CBS affiliate, but the local ABC station carried selected CBS shows, including both *Gunsmoke* and *Have Gun Will Travel*. Unfortunately, *Rawhide* was not available until its final season, which meant scrambling to the house of a friend or relative with an antenna strong enough to capture the CBS signal from Madison, Wisconsin, or Chicago. As this was not always possible, I did not see the series in its entirety until it went into syndication. Not expecting much more than some sentimental viewing, I was very gratified to discover that *Rawhide* was better than I remembered, and with the advent of the VCR era I began recording the show whenever I could. Like virtually all syndicated series, the episodes were edited (sometimes carelessly) to allow for more commercials, so the fifty uncut installments CBS's Columbia House subsidiary released on home video in the early 1990s were most welcome. (Currently, the first three seasons are available on DVD from CBS/Paramount Home Video.)

With its large ensemble of perfectly cast characters, rugged settings and frequently exceptional writing, *Rawhide* continues to transcend mere nostalgia and is definitely worthy of examination. Several years ago a book about the show was said to be in the works, but now, more than two decades later, it has yet to appear. I hope any readers who were anticipating that project will find this proverbial labor of love a worthy alternative.

David R. Greenland

INTRODUCTION

During an appearance on David Letterman's *Late Show* in early 2007, Clint Eastwood seemed genuinely amazed when the studio audience burst into enthusiastic applause at Letterman's mention of *Rawhide*. "That was so long ago" said Eastwood, grinning widely. "But it was a good show."

True, it had been more than forty years since the final first-run episode was broadcast, but fans of classic television series tend to have long memories, and *Rawhide* is unquestionably a classic. Not only "a good show," but for most of its eight-season run a *great* show, one of only a very few television Westerns capable of authenticity as well as imagination. It was also unique in capturing the vast scope of the wilderness west of the Mississippi river more successfully than any other series, including *Wagon Train*, to which it was frequently compared. Most shows in the genre took place in towns or on ranches, often resulting in monotony or mediocrity. Before becoming familiar with the characters and willing to accept them in any setting, *Rawhide* viewers objected to episodes that were town-bound, and did not hesitate to let the network know it. Consequently, filming was done at a wide variety of locations, both within and outside of California (Arizona, New Mexico, Oklahoma, Texas), giving the series a more credible look than many others. Even when shooting around the Los Angeles area, most familiar sites—such as Bronson Canyon, Thousand Oaks, Big Sky Ranch, Red Rock Canyon, Lone Pine, Chinese Camp, to name only half a dozen of at least that many more—were used sparingly, or at least as creatively as possible. Several private ranches were also rented, and filming on phony studio exteriors was often restricted to night scenes, where a degree of realism could be achieved.

Although *Rawhide* employed its share of familiar faces from Hollywood's past (Brian Donlevy, Mary Astor, Peter Lorre, Barbara Stanwyck, Claude Rains and Lon Chaney, Jr., among them), its large and colorful cast usually ensured that guest stars did not often hog the spotlight and detract from the overall tone of the show.

Rawhide debuted in January 1959, the peak of the Western on television, and was one of fifteen such series introduced that year, including such stalwarts as *Bonanza, Laramie* and *The Rebel.* Up to then, sixty-seven others had been produced for either syndicated or network broadcast since 1949, none of them depicting the struggle between Man and Mother Nature as regularly or as excitingly as *Rawhide.* Western fans who complained that most shows were mostly talk and little action overlooked the fact that many of these programs were better written and acted than such beloved yet rather simple-minded efforts as *The Gene Autry Show, The Roy Rogers Show, Hopalong Cassidy* or *The Lone Ranger.* In retrospect, *Rawhide* stands nearly alone in its ability to combine intriguing stories, believable dialogue and large doses of usually uncontrived adventure.

Despite the prominence and popularity of Westerns, the Television Academy of Arts and Sciences, like the Motion Picture Academy, gave them little respect. Literally dozens of outstanding performances and scripts were ignored year after year. For the 1959 season, when the genre was at its peak, the sole Western-related Emmy nomination was for Richard Boone's portrayal of Paladin on *Have Gun Will Travel.* Evidently the Television Academy felt it had paid the genre token recognition the previous year with a record seven nominations (two wins). *Rawhide* was never noticed, obviously dismissed as nothing but another "horse opera." As an unidentified network executive remarked in 1959, "The Western is just the neatest and quickest type of escape entertainment, that's all."

While *Rawhide*'s popularity fluctuated, it ranked among the top thirty programs for five of its eight seasons, and is the fourth longest-running Western of all time, ranking behind *Gunsmoke, Bonanza* and *The Virginian* (*Rawhide* is reduced to number five by viewers who consider *Little House on the Prairie*—a frontier drama set in Minnesota—a Western. Technically, *Rawhide* shares its position with *Wagon Train,* which also lasted for eight seasons). And while it was shut out of Emmy consideration, two episodes were nominated for an Eddy award by the American Cinema Editors (winning one) and *Rawhide* was among the Golden Globe nominees for Best Television Show of 1963. More significantly, from 1961 to 1965, four scripts earned the Western Heritage Award for fictional television drama from the Cowboy and Western Heritage Museum.

The challenges *Rawhide* endured were numerous and included two of the most crucial any television series can face: changes in the regular cast and scheduling. In addition, the show was moved to four different studios and was guided by at least five different producers, each with their own vision of what direction *Rawhide* should take. In retrospect, it is impressive to note that the series maintained a generally high level of quality throughout its time on the air, with most of the lesser moments occurring in only the last two years.

The definite history of *Rawhide*, sadly, can never be written. Too many regular cast members, guest stars, producers, directors, writers and stunt people are no longer among the living. The purpose of this book is to not only pay tribute to *Rawhide*, but to gather in one place all the widely scattered information about the show and provide as many new revelations as possible. This is also an opportunity to correct errors in *Rawhide*'s generally accepted story (much of it on the Internet), such as the total number of episodes being given as 144 in more than one reference book. There were, in fact, 217. Similarly, the date of the last network broadcast (January 4, 1966) was a rerun, not the final first-run episode, which aired December 17, 1965. And while *Rawhide* did not resort to using as many big name guest stars as other series, there were exceptions. Sammy Davis, Jr., however, was not one of them.

In the immortal words of trail boss Gil Favor—who did not, contrary to some sources, quote from his journal at the beginning of every episode—*now is the time to head 'em up and move 'em out.*

PART ONE

CHAPTER ONE
HEAD 'EM UP

By the time *Rawhide* creator/producer Charles Marquis Warren turned twenty one in December of 1955 he had been a football star at Baltimore City College and written a play ("No Sun, No Moon") that was not only produced at Princeton University but also optioned for filming by Hollywood studio Metro-Goldwyn-Mayer. As if that were not enough success for such a young man, Warren's godfather was able to secure a staff writing position for him at MGM, specifically adapting the novel *Tender is the Night* for filming. It did not hurt that his godfather happened to be the novel's author, the legendary F. Scott Fitzgerald, who was to take a few stabs at screenwriting himself, contributing to the scripts for *A Yank at Oxford* (1938), *Gone with the Wind* (1939), and a few others. Fitzgerald once advised his daughter to ask herself: "What am I really aiming at?" It is not known if he offered the same guidance to his godson, but Warren eventually concluded that the screen trade was not his goal. At least not yet. Instead, he moved to New York and began writing pulp fiction, primarily Westerns. Two of his stories, "Only the Valiant" and "Valley of the Shadow," were serialized in *The Saturday Evening Post* and later published as books.

When World War II broke out, Warren enlisted in the Navy and rose to the rank of commander. Toward the end of the war, as he supervised the filming of an amphibious landing on a Japanese-held island, he was wounded. While recuperating in the hospital, he learned that Warner Bros. had purchased the rights to his novel *Only the Valiant*, though it was not produced until 1951. Starring Gregory Peck and future *Wagon Train* lead Ward Bond, the film's cast included no less than six actors—Neville Brand, Lon Chaney Jr., Jeff Corey, Michael Ansara, Steve Brodie, Hugh Sanders—who would later appear in episodes of *Rawhide*. During his career, Warren's fondness for certain actors with whom he worked was known to have a direct bearing on the show's casting decisions, regular members as well as guests.

After the war, Warren, who was known as "Bill" to his friends, returned to Hollywood and once again pursued the art of screenwriting. His first credit, *Beyond Glory*, starring Alan Ladd as a World War II veteran accused of misconduct, was released in 1948. The following year, he collaborated with two other writers on *Streets of Laredo*, a remake of 1936's *The Texas Rangers*, starring William Holden and Macdonald Carey. After that, Warren must have known what he was, in Fitzgerald's words, "really aiming at," because the majority of his creative endeavors from then on were almost exclusively Westerns.

At Paramount Pictures, Warren assisted two other writers in adapting his novel *The Redhead and the Cowboy* for a 1950 film starring Glenn Ford and Rhonda Fleming. Regrettably, Ms. Fleming's flaming tresses were seen only in black-and-white.

In 1951, after writing *The Fighting Coast Guard* (starring *Rawhide* guests Brian Donlevy, Forrest Tucker and Steve Brodie), he both co-wrote and directed *Little Big Horn* for Robert L. Lippert Productions. The modest but effective film starred Lloyd Bridges and a supporting cast populated almost entirely of future *Rawhide* guests, including Marie Windsor, Reed Hadley, Jim Davis, Noah Beery, Jr. (billed as Noah Berry), Rodd Redwing, King Donovan and, most notably, Sheb Wooley and John Ireland. The same year he found time to write *Oh! Susanna*, starring Rod Cameron, Jim Davis, Douglas Kennedy, Chill Wills and Forrest Tucker (all but Rod Cameron would be on *Rawhide*) for Republic Pictures. Cameron also starred in Republic's *Woman of the North Country*, co-written by Warren, the following year.

Moving to Warner Bros., Warren co-wrote the 1952 Gary Cooper vehicle *Springfield Rifle*, and then formed Commander Films Corporation, for which he co-wrote and directed *Hellgate*, starring Sterling Hayden, Ward Bond and a little-known actor named James Arness.

The next year, Warren went back to Paramount to co-write *Pony Express* as well as co-write and direct *Arrowhead*, both starring Charlton Heston. Among the cast of the latter was character actor Milburn Stone, later to be uncomfortably reunited with Warren on *Gunsmoke*. Before the year was over, Warren stepped outside the Western genre to write and direct *Flight to Tangiers*, featuring *Arrowhead* co-star Jack Palance.

Seven Angry Men, directed by Warren for Allied Artists and released in 1955, starred Raymond Massey and featured yet another roster of *Rawhide* guests: Deborah Paget, James Best, James Anderson, Dabbs Greer, Leo Gordon and John Pickard. Most significantly, the cast included Dennis Weaver, who would be portraying Chester Goode on *Gunsmoke* before the year was out.

Gunsmoke, incidentally, would consume the lion's share of Charles Marquis Warren's time and creativity for almost two years. Initially he was reluctant to take the CBS network's offer to develop the popular radio program for television, a medium he held in low regard. He admitted that he did not even own a television. CBS persisted, dangling an offer of seven thousand dollars a month—in those days, *big* money that Warren knew he would be foolish to turn down. The network gave him free rein—to the great disappointment of Gunsmoke's creators, writer John Meston and producer Norman Macdonnell—though they remained involved with the series. In short order, Warren took over casting, altering the characters of Matt Dillon, Doc Adams, Kitty Russell and Chester Goode from how they had been portrayed on radio. He also influenced the tone and look of the show, right down to the wardrobe. Feeling *Gunsmoke* sounded too much like a B movie, he proposed changing the title to *The Outrider*, which CBS correctly vetoed on the grounds that it made no sense to switch an already familiar brand.

For anyone who has wondered why the titles of the *Rawhide* episodes produced during the series' first three seasons (and even later) began with the word "Incident," the most likely explanation can be found in the instructions Warren gave to the *Gunsmoke* writers: "Let's not do stories—let's do incidents."

During the first season, Warren penned four scripts based on John Meston's radio plays, came up with one original story ("Night Incident") and, in addition to functioning as producer, directed twenty-six of thirty-nine episodes. Understandably burned out by the time work began on the second season, he produced only thirteen episodes before passing the torch to associate producer Norman Macdonnell. Warren was also tired of bickering with the cast—Arness and Stone in particular—about how their characters should be played, and anxious to begin other projects.

Warren wrote the story for a proposed Sheb Wooley series entitled *Cavalry Patrol*, but when the pilot did not sell he returned to features, directing Richard Egan and Dorothy Malone in 1956's *Tension at Table Rock* for RKO Radio Pictures.

Possibly the busiest—or at least the most varied—year of Warren's career was 1957. He directed two low budget horror films (*Back from the Dead* and *The Unknown Terror*, with casts featuring such eventual *Rawhide* guests as Arthur Franz, Paul Richards and Mala Powers) before returning to familiar territory for the United Artists Western *Trooper Hook*, starring Joel McCrea, Barbara Stanwyck and the reliable Sheb Wooley. Wooley also appeared in two films Warren directed for Fox: *The Black Whip* (with Hugh Marlowe, Colleen Gray and Paul Richards) and *Ride a Violent Mile* (with John Agar and John Pickard). Somehow he found time to write an episode of the CBS anthology series *Playhouse 90* and be the executive producer of Fox's *Copper Sky*, starring Jeff Morrow, Colleen Gray and a diminutive but distinctive character actor by the name of Paul Brinegar.

Warren began 1958 by directing Brian Keith in *Desert Hell*, a foreign legion adventure, and the Western *Blood Arrow*, starring Scott Brady and three *Rawhide* alumni (Phyllis Coates, Don Haggerty and Paul Richards).

Of greater significance was *Cattle Empire*, the Joel McCrea color epic he produced and directed for Fox. As early as 1955, Warren had pitched the idea for a series about cattle drovers, but CBS and the other networks turned it down. *Cattle Empire*, not to be confused with the somewhat superior *Cattle Drive* that McCrea had made seven years earlier (nor with 1952's *Cattle Town*, with Sheb Wooley), was Warren's attempt to scratch that particular creative itch. Endre Bohem, one of the film's three writers, had co-written the final episode of *Gunsmoke* produced by Warren, and would be a major contributor to the development and success of *Rawhide*. Not surprisingly, *Cattle Empire* co-starred future *Rawhide* guests Gloria Talbott, Don Haggerty and Phyllis Coates. Yet the supporting cast seems more important today: Paul Brinegar, Steve Raines, Rocky Shahan and Charles Gray were all destined to become *Rawhide* regulars.

Evidently Richard Sparks, a veteran producer who by 1958 was running CBS's filmed programming division, was suitably impressed by *Cattle Empire* to give Warren and Endre Bohem, initially credited as story editor, the green light to shoot a series pilot. Almost immediately, Warren ran into network opposition. He wanted to cast only one leading actor; CBS said no, there also had to be a younger second lead on the order of John Wayne and Montgomery Clift in the trail drive cinematic classic *Red River* from nine years before. Even bolder was Warren's request that the series be expanded to ninety minutes; certainly not, the network responded. This was just another Western, not a prestigious dramatic TV anthology like *Playhouse 90*. For the title, Warren once again suggested naming the show *The Outrider*, or *Outriders*, now that there were to be two top stars. And once again the network rejected it. Specifically, CBS founder and Chairman William S. Paley gave the idea thumbs down, saying he much preferred the Western-sounding *Rawhide*, also the title of a well done and very popular Tyrone Power picture from 1951. Furthermore, Paley reasoned, the name of NBC's new hit *Wagon Train* was a logical extension of director John Ford's *Wagonmaster*. And *Wagon Train* was winning the ratings race against both CBS and ABC on Wednesday night. There was a lot to be said for the power of audience identification. Knowing that there was no way to make the pilot without going along with the network's demands, Warren resigned himself to creating a sixty-minute show called *Rawhide*, headed by two actors sharing top billing.

While *Red River* was an obvious template, the series was also inspired by a journal kept by cattleman George Duffield, who in 1866 drove a herd of longhorns from Texas to Iowa. Duffield recorded a litany of hazards encountered on the drive, from bad weather and illness to discouraged drovers and menacing Indians of the Comanche and Kiowa tribes, all of which would provide Warren and his writers with story ideas.

From an actual historical perspective, *Rawhide* was generally on the mark. Bad winter weather in 1863 forced as many as six million cattle into southern Texas by the end of the Civil War. To meet the Eastern demand for beef, Confederate veterans began rounding them up driving the herds north, to railheads in Kansas. From 1867 through 1871, the chief destination for well over one million longhorns was Abilene, the end of the famed Chisholm Trail, where cattle pens could accommodate 120,000 head in a season. Another trail was the Shawnee, running from San Antonio, Texas, to Sedalia, Missouri. Many drives chose this route after 1871, when Kansas expanded the quarantine line, a boundary intended to keep Texas ticks out of the state. Oddly, Texas longhorns, descended from herds brought to North America from Spain, were immune to the fever these insects caused in other cattle.

With this rich vein of history to mine, Warren assigned the task of writing the pilot to *Gunsmoke* veteran Les Crutchfield. Hiring a cast and arranging the logistics of the production did not take long, and by April 5, 1958, *TV Guide* was reporting that "CBS will shoot it out against NBC's *Wagon Train* with another hour-long Western next fall. *Rawhide* moves into the Wednesday night at 7:30 (ET) spot, to be followed by Arthur Godfrey's *Talent Scouts* at 8:30."

Fate had other plans.

CHAPTER TWO
Eric Fleming
(Gil Favor, Trail Boss)

Charles Marquis Warren once described Eric Fleming as "a miserable human being." Even after achieving worldwide fame as Gil Favor, Fleming referred to himself as "bitter" and "twisted." Considering the hellish childhood and disfiguring facial injury he experienced before becoming an actor, these assessments are understandable.

A complex, even mysterious man, he was born Edward Heddy Jr. on July 4, 1925, in Santa Paula, a community in California's Ventura County. (In later years Fleming would claim he was not sure of either his birth date or place.) *Rawhide* would film extensively at Big Sky Ranch, also located in Ventura County, but it is doubtful that Fleming ever felt the urge to visit Santa Paula. His father, Edward F. Heddy Sr., was a twenty-eight-year-old occasional oil worker, originally from New York. His Minnesota-born mother, Mildred Anderson Heddy, was also twenty-eight. The future Gil Favor was the Heddys' only child.

By the time he was six, Fleming was hawking newspapers while his father worked infrequently as a carpenter. Heddy Sr., an abusive sort, had little use for his son, once beating him so severely that Fleming was bedridden for at least a couple of days. When the boy was hospitalized for six weeks with a bone condition known as osteomyelitis, his father never visited. During his recovery, Fleming's father continued to beat him and allegedly went so far as to chain his son in the basement. The fact that the boy was using crutches to get around made no difference.

In 1934, just shy of his ninth birthday, Fleming attempted to shoot his father, but the gun jammed. Rather than try again, he, like innumerable desperate Depression era citizens, hitched a ride on a freight train bound for Los Angeles, eventually making his way to Chicago. There, he led a threadbare existence, often doing odd jobs for underworld types. This association with gangsters resulted in his being wounded in a gun battle and landing back in the hospital. Authorities returned Fleming, then eleven, to his parents, who had recently separated. When California police observed how fearful he was of his father, they took him to live with his mother.

Fleming regarded himself as generally ugly, with a nose too large for his face and a club that required him to wear a brace on his right leg. Consequently, he was withdrawn and insecure, skipping school more often than not and never graduating. Following a series of low paying jobs that included waiting tables and working construction, Fleming joined the Merchant Marines and discovered a love of the sea.

In 1942, looking older than his seventeen years, he lied about his age and joined the Navy, becoming a Seabee and building airfields and bases of operation in the South Pacific. While stationed in Seattle, he bet a group of sailors ten dollars that he could hoist a two hundred pound steel block above his head. Fleming succeeded, but the line slipped and the block smashed into his face. Navy plastic surgeons performed four separate operations to reconstruct his jaw, forehead and, in Fleming's estimation, his oversized nose. (His original face can be seen in a naval training film produced in 1944.) Many years later, as he prepared to take on the role of Gil Favor, he confided to a reporter that because he was never even remotely handsome before the accident, his main concern had been losing an eye. "I had no idea I'd end up looking like this," he added. "I've learned that it's give and take all the way, and I have before and after advantages, which gives a wonderful balance of values."

Fleming evidently continued to embrace a down to earth outlook on life, living in what was once a garage during the *Rawhide* years. "I've lived out of a paper bag all my life," he remarked a year after leaving the series.

Military duty behind him, Fleming found work as a laborer at Hollywood's Paramount Studios in 1946. Although he contemplated becoming a writer—and would later collaborate on two *Rawhide* scripts—he also remembered a few of his fellow sailors suggesting that with his new face he should give acting a try. He bet an aspiring actor $100 that he could ace an audition, but lost.

Undaunted, he changed his name from Edward Heddy Jr. to Eric Fleming and began taking acting lessons at night. By 1948 he was working with the West Coast company of *Happy Birthday*, starring Miriam Hopkins, known chiefly for such classic films as the 1932 version of *Dr. Jekyll and Mr. Hyde* and *Old Acquaintance* (1943). The play moved to Broadway, where he sustained himself on a diet consisting largely of scrambled eggs.

Early in 1951, he made his television debut as the title character in the series *Major Dell Conway of the Flying Tigers* on the DuMont network. The first episodes aired from April 7 to May 26, and when the show resumed in July for an eight-month run, it was as a syndicated series renamed *The Flying Tigers*. And Fleming had been replaced by Ed Peck.

For the next couple of years he struggled, finding work on the stage (*Stalag 17, My Three Angels*) and on such television programs as NBC's *Cameo Theater* ("Dark of the Moon") and *Hallmark Hall of Fame* ("Joan of Arc," "The General's Bible," "To My Valentine").

While appearing on Broadway in Jose Ferrer's production of *My Three Angels*, he was spotted by representatives from his old employer, Paramount, and offered the lead in science fiction producer George Pal's film *Conquest of Space*, to be directed by Byron Haskin. *War of the Worlds* (1953), Pal and Haskin's most recent effort, had been a tremendous hit, so Fleming had reason to be optimistic. He accepted the role and in 1954 was back in Hollywood.

Conquest of Space benefited from admirable special effects and a good supporting cast, including Ross Martin and future *Rawhide* guest star Walter Burke, but was sunk by an inferior script. By December, Fleming was back on Broadway, co-starring with Jennifer Jones in *Portrait of a Lady*.

After more stage work in *No Time for Sergeants* and *Teahouse of the August Moon*, he made his second film, playing a psychiatrist opposite Nancy Malone in the forgotten thriller *Fright*, a 1956 release also known as *Spell of the Hypnotist*. That same year he returned to television in episodes of *Hollywood Summer Theatre* and *The Phil Silvers Show*, both on CBS.

In one of the few interviews conducted with him during this period, Fleming spoke of his unhappy youth, revealing that he had seen his father only once since leaving home. They never saw each other again.

His acting opportunities were sparse in 1957, limited to a guest role on NBC's anthology *Suspicion* ("Heartbeat") and his third film, the campy *Queen of Outer Space*, starring Zsa Zsa Gabor and released the next year.

Following an installment of CBS's highly regarded *Studio One* ("The Strong Man"), Fleming appeared in his first Western, *Curse of the Undead*, made in 1958 but not released until after *Rawhide* began airing in early 1959. Shot entirely on the back lot of Universal Studio, the odd film could easily have been entitled "Dracula Out West." Fleming played a preacher and was not given much to do for the first twenty minutes, nor did he get to strap on a gun until the final five, but he projected confidence among a sturdy cast that included Michael Pate, Kathleen Crowley and John Hoyt, all destined to appear in episodes of *Rawhide*.

Frustrated by a career that (in his view) was going nowhere, Fleming seriously considered giving up acting and moving to the South Pacific to take a long-delayed stab at writing. As the summer of 1958 began, he was on the verge of leaving Hollywood when his agent informed him that auditions were being held for a new CBS Western series. Aware that Westerns were currently the most popular programs on television, and that two of the best—*Gunsmoke* and *Have Gun-Will Travel*—were on CBS, Fleming figured it made sense to take a chance, most likely his last.

At CBS' Television City, he was asked to perform a lengthy monologue. Fortuitously, Fleming possessed a photographic memory and was able to master a page of script after a single reading. It was, however, an ability he did not have to utilize very often once the series got underway, and not only because he grew to feel he was worthy of superior material. "Fleming was stiff," said Charles Larson, writer of a dozen *Rawhide* episodes. "We were always told not to make his speeches in his scenes with other people too long. We had to write in short breaks in the other person's speech so Fleming would have a line. If he had to just stand there and react, he felt jumpy. He didn't know what to do."

Ted Post, director of twenty episodes, thought Fleming had a tendency to overact and sometimes found it necessary to instruct him to tone down his delivery. This could very well explain Fleming's frequent tight lipped, monotone reading of his lines. He never claimed to be a first rate actor, often telling reporters that all his co-stars—even the horses—were better thespians. "These guys can act," he once said. "I am just a hack." Co-star Charles Gray disagreed, saying, "Eric did a hell of a job as Gil Favor."

Nonetheless, the Gil Favor character, with his rumbling baritone and firm air of authority, quickly became an audience favorite, garnering the 6' 4" Fleming a majority of the show's fan mail. In addition, he was the sole cast member to be immortalized with a figurine by Hartland Plastics, which manufactured a line of television cowboys (and their horses) in the early 1960s.

Fleming's character was also the only one to be given a substantial back story, that of a former Confederate captain whose wife had died, leaving him with two young daughters who were seen in a pair of memorable episodes, along with Favor's sister-in-law.

Although he is warmly remembered by friends and several guest stars, many among the regular cast considered Fleming aloof and reclusive. Between camera set-ups he would often retreat to his dressing room or bury himself in a book. "He loved to shock people [with] radical statements—annoy a lot of people," Clint Eastwood recalled.

A rare glimpse of a jovial Fleming occurred when he, Eastwood, Paul Brinegar, and actress Ruta Lee made a 1962 appearance on the CBS game show *Stump the Stars.*

John Hart, who appeared in seventeen episodes, occasionally as a bespectacled drover created by Endre Bohem and known only as Narbo, said of Fleming, "He was a nice enough guy. There was a funny thing about him. He wouldn't wear shoes. He'd go to a black tie party for a premiere, he'd have on a beautiful tuxedo and he'd be barefooted."

Fleming's penchant for going barefoot, even on strolls down Sunset Boulevard, was never explained definitively. It has been attributed to everything from his eccentric nature ("He was a bit eccentric," said Charles Gary, "but so are most actors") or an affinity acquired while stationed in the Pacific, to pain in his club foot or a simple foot fungus.

Eric Fleming.

"Eric was pretty much of a loner," remembered Sheb Wooley. "He was athletic, played tennis. A nice man, but a little different. He didn't like to shake hands with anybody, afraid he'd pick up germs. If he liked you or respected you, you got along just fine with him. You never expected a lot of warmth, but he was honest. You might not like what he had to say, but he was honest about it."

Professionally, Fleming was always on a collision course with Charles Marquis Warren, whose dictatorial style and unpredictable work schedule irritated most people associated with *Rawhide*. Fleming, however, was the only one who either staged periodic strikes or vowed to quit the series entirely. His participation in some episodes was minimal, and there were times Favor was completely absent, viewers being informed that he was off selling cattle to the army or buying stock from ranches along the trail. "He was perfectly willing to take time off," said Paul Brinegar. "He was glad when he was written down in an episode."

After one of Fleming's walk-outs, Warren, fed up with his star's behavior, told the press that Fleming was being replaced by Gregory Walcott, who would eventually make five guest appearances as different characters on the show. In reality, Warren had no intention of hiring Walcott—even though the actor did an extensive screen test for the role of *Rawhide's* new trail boss—and was merely using him to scare Fleming into returning. The ploy worked. Walcott did not learn the truth until years later.

Of Warren, Fleming reflected after leaving the show, "I love him. But I loved fifty other men who were trying to make a living and he'd come in at 6 p.m., ready to work when everybody was ready to quit." Fleming demanded a six o'clock quitting time and got it, much to the relief of the cast and crew, but continued to clash with the long line of executives who succeeded Warren.

During his last season, he disagreed with the direction the show was taking, which included a growing emphasis on Eastwood's character, and angrily confronted story editor Del Reisman. "I'm gonna walk out on this. If there's any legal action, you go ahead and take my house. I don't give a damn."

By this time, 1964, Fleming had been the first of several actors (Charles Bronson, Rory Calhoun and James Coburn among them) approached to star in Italian director Sergio Leone's *A Fistful of*

Dollars, but he turned the offer down, recommending Eastwood instead. Perhaps to repay Fleming's thoughtfulness, Eastwood spoke up when he learned that executive producer Ben Brady planned to eliminate the Gil Favor character from the cast prior to what would be *Rawhide*'s final season. "You mean fire the wrong guy? Keep Fleming and get rid of me. You don't really need me. I would prefer to be out of the show." Eastwood was in the process of making a second film for Leone (*For a Few Dollars More*) and was not anxious to return to the grind of weekly television.

As it turned out, Eastwood was right: Brady did fire "the wrong guy." Without Gil Favor, *Rawhide* did not have long to live. The show was past its peak of popularity even before Fleming's last season, but his absence was doubtlessly a major reason it never finished its final drive.

Initially, Brady had offered Fleming an improved financial deal if he would remain with the series, but their negotiations failed. "Mr. Favor" had moved his last herd. Fleming claimed the reason he was let go was the network's refusal to pay him one million dollars per season. In truth, he was being paid $220,000, very good money in 1965. There were also murmurings that CBS was not pleased to learn that he had signed to do a Doris Day comedy before his network contract expired.

The movie, *The Glass Bottom Boat*, was filmed in Hawaii, where Fleming purchased a ranch and intended to retire. He was billed seventh, playing a spy posing as CIA agent "Edgar Hill" and did not appear until nearly half an hour into the film. "You can't imagine how pleasant it is to work with a washed face and have a rug under your feet," he told a reporter. "There is something deadly about working for six years with a male cast."

As difficult as he could be, Fleming evidently had no problem getting along with the opposite sex. He in fact dated more than a few actresses who worked on *Rawhide*, including Carol Byron, Abby Dalton, Olive Sturges and Kipp Hamilton. He was also seen with Marilyn Fix, daughter of actor Paul Fix ("Micah Torrence" on *The Rifleman*) and the future wife of actor Harry Carey Jr. Another woman he was involved with was writer Chris Miller, who co-wrote Fleming's two *Rawhide* scripts; at the time of his death he was engaged to actress Lynn Garber.

Michael Landon and Fleming in "Peace Officer" episode of *Bonanza*.

Rumors that Fleming was being considered for the part of Captain Kirk on *Star Trek* have never been verified, but in late 1965 he returned to television, effective as a sadistic lawman in "Peace Officer," an episode of *Bonanza* which aired February 6, 1966. That same month, he remarked, "I don't want to act anymore. I'd like to become a teacher. I was never a great actor. I never expected to be. I'd like to settle down on the beach in Hawaii." He still had the writing bug and also wanted to try his hand at painting and sculpting.

Before exploring these avenues, Fleming headed to Lone Pine, California, in the summer of 1966 to film "The Pursued," a two-part episode of *Bonanza* directed by Western veteran William Witney. Fleming's portrayal of Heber Clauson, a Mormon horse rancher with two wives, was, like his other *Bonanza* appearance, quite unlike Gil Favor, and many of his admirers rate it his finest performance. "It was also the last thing he ever did," recalled *Bonanza* creator/executive producer David Dortort. Part one was broadcast on October 2. By then Fleming, age forty-one, had been dead for nearly a week. Eerily, he had told more than one person that he felt he would die young.

In the late summer of 1966, Fleming was back in the 19th century—though not in the saddle—when he took on the role of a naval officer in "High Jungle," a two-part installment of ABC's anthology series *Off to See the Wizard*, set to debut in the fall. He flew to Lima, Peru, on August 17, accompanied by Lynn Garber. After several weeks of filming, the production moved to the remote jungle of the Amazon Basin, more than two hundred miles from Lima.

On September 28, with a thunderstorm brewing and the cast and crew anxious to return to civilization, Fleming and co-star Nico Minardos prepared to shoot the final location scene in a thirty-five foot dugout canoe on the raging Huallaga River. It was a dangerous sequence that, in retrospect, should have been performed by experienced stunt doubles, but the actors felt up to the challenge. They shoved off and, barely a minute later, hit a stretch of rapids that began to swamp the primitive vessel. Fleming either jumped or fell into the water, while Minardos managed to stay with the canoe until rescued. Attempts to reach Fleming failed, and the crew could only watch helplessly as he was carried downriver in the churning rapids.

Conflicting accounts as to when Fleming's body was eventually discovered range from a few days to almost a week. Similarly, the disposition of his remains is unclear. According to his will, his body was to be donated to science, yet he was at one time reported to be buried in a South American cemetery. Other sources stated that his remains went either to the University of San Marcas in Lima, or the UCLA Medical Center in Los Angeles. In reality, Fleming was most likely devoured by piranhas, a fact confirmed by more than one member of the search team that found his body.

For some reason news of his demise was slow to reach the press; Clint Eastwood did not learn of his former co-star's death until November 1. And reports sanitized the circumstances, saying that he had simply drowned.

Although Fleming willed most of his $125,000 estate to his mother, he left ten thousand each to Lynn Garber, Chris Miller and a cousin. His father, not surprisingly, was cut out completely.

The tragic death of Eric Fleming was a sad finale to a life spent largely in discontent. Yet despite how he may have regarded his role on *Rawhide*, he continues to live in reruns and on home video as one of the more memorable fictional characters in television history—Gil Favor, Trail Boss.

CHAPTER THREE
CLINT EASTWOOD
(ROWDY YATES, RAMROD)

So much has been written about Clint Eastwood over the past forty-plus years—including no less than four often contradictory and error-filled biographies—that he is doubtlessly a leading candidate for most well known private person on the globe. Although he has referred to the character of Rowdy Yates as "Idiot of the Plains," he has also conceded that Rawhide is responsible for his status as an international film star and a two-time Academy Award winning director.

The future Rowdy was born May 31, 1930, in Oakland, California, to Clinton Eastwood Sr. and the former Margaret Ruth Runner, who were married two years before. The Eastwoods made the first of several moves along the West Coast shortly after Clint Junior's birth, his father finding employment as a service station attendant, banker, bond salesman, and at a jewelry company before settling in Piedmont, California, for eight years. When World War II broke out, Eastwood Sr. took a job as a pipefitter in a shipyard so he could remain close to his family, which now included daughter Jeanne, born in 1934. After his son had become a television star, and until his death in July 1970, the elder Eastwood was affectionately called "Rawhide" by many of his friends and business acquaintances.

Young Clint spent a considerable amount of time at his maternal grandmother's ranch, giving him his first exposure to cowboy life. Ironically, he discovered that he was allergic to horses, a condition which obviously did not affect the upward trajectory of his career.

By the time he entered high school, Eastwood was a tall, shy, good looking kid with a friendly grin. He also tended to be something of a loner whose fondness for music leaned more toward jazz than country or pop. (In later life he would contribute to the soundtracks of several of his films, and direct a biography of saxophonist Charlie Parker, as well as documentaries about pianist Thelonious Monk and the great Ray Charles. During the *Rawhide* years, the legendary trumpeter Miles Davis asked Eastwood for autographs for his sons, who were fans of the show.) An English teacher pressured him and another student to stage a one-act play, which he briefly considered skipping out on. Several of his fellow students complimented him on his performance, but he found the experience uncomfortable. "I don't ever want to do that again, ever in life!" he insisted.

Eastwood held a variety of jobs before turning twenty-one, including pumping gas, tending bar and logging. He wanted to enroll at Seattle University and study music, but was drafted in 1951 and sent to Fort Ord. After basic training, he was assigned to be a lifeguard and swimming instructor at the base pool. His swimming skills soon proved vital when a plane he was riding in had to make a forced landing in the rough waters of the Pacific.

In 1953, the service behind him, he married Maggie Johnson and enrolled in Los Angeles City College on the G.I. Bill, intending to major in business administration. Instead, he decided to take acting classes, eventually being accepted into Universal-International Studio's training program, never earning more than $75 a week. He was scratched from the studio payroll in September 1955 after having only bit parts in eight films. Some of these included the science-fiction classics *Revenge of the Creature* and *Tarantula*, the comedy *Francis in the Navy*, the war picture *Away All Boats*, and his first Western, *Star in the Dust*, in which he played a nameless ranch hand. He was also nameless and nearly impossible to spot in "The Charles Avery Story," an episode of *Wagon Train*, its production company based at Universal.

For the next couple of years, in spite of being favorably compared to Gary Cooper and James Dean, Eastwood found little acting work and at one point was reduced to digging swimming pools. He appeared in episodes of *The Steve Allen Show, Highway Patrol, West Point, Navy Log* and *Death Valley Days*, all of which paid next to nothing. He did, however, appear in two theatrical Westerns, RKO's *The*

First Traveling Saleslady (1956, with James Arness) and Regal's *Ambush at Cimarron Pass*, released by 20th Century-Fox in 1958, each offering more screen time than he had been given at Universal. In the latter, a low budget production, Eastwood overacted to amusing effect, throwing a fit anytime the word "Yankee" was uttered.

Bill Shiffrin, Eastwood's agent, heard that CBS was planning another Western series and that while the lead was intended for an older actor, other roles still needed to be cast. Eastwood, along with his friend Sonia Chernus, a former story editor at Universal, went to CBS Television City and "accidentally" ran into the network's Robert Sparks, in charge of programming. Sparks invited Eastwood to meet with him and producer Charles Marquis Warren, whom Eastwood would later remember as "wearing old clothes. Looked like he'd just been pushing a broom in the back room. I didn't know whether he was going to sweep under the chair or what." An awkward silence filled the room when the young actor greeted Warren as "Bill," a name used by only the veteran producer's closest friends. Nevertheless, Warren asked Eastwood to audition, on camera and in full Western garb, the following day. For the screen test, Warren handed him a sheet containing one of Henry Fonda's speeches from *The Ox Bow Incident*. Eastwood was not a quick study and forgot most of the words, opting to give a sense of the scene, more or less. While looking over the material he had overheard another actor do a letter perfect reading, and left figuring he had no chance at getting the role. Industry scuttlebutt was that Bing Russell (father of Kurt and destined to portray deputy Clem Foster on *Bonanza*) had the inside advantage, having previously worked for Warren.

However, a week later, Shiffrin called and said that one of the CBS executives, Hubbell Robinson, had seen all the screen tests insisted Eastwood looked best. ("That's the guy. I don't need to see anyone else. I like him.") The part was his, although the character had no name as yet. According John Dunkel, writer of twenty *Rawhide* scripts, he was meeting with story editor Endre Bohem when Warren stopped by to announce that he "had a name for the sidekick: Rowdy." Eastwood was signed to the series for a salary of seven hundred dollars a week, a kingly sum in 1958, especially for a mostly out of work actor.

The character of Rowdy Yates was a young former Confederate soldier who had done time in a Union prison and was now a ramrod, second in command on a cattle drive. Even though Eastwood had been told the leading role would belong to an older actor, he and Eric Fleming had a disagreement about whose show it was on the very first day of shooting. Fleming also complained that the young actor was speaking his lines too slowly. Some witnesses claimed the dispute erupted in fisticuffs; others contend it *almost* went that way. Most accounts have the two actors leaving the set to settle the matter privately. In any event, Fleming and Eastwood were able to smooth things over and work compatibly for seven seasons, but, Eastwood has said, "We were never close friends."

During the summer of 1958, anywhere from six to ten episodes (sources vary) of *Rawhide* were shot on location in Arizona and California and at Universal, before CBS opted not to include the series on its prime time schedule. That fall there were already more than twenty-five Westerns slated for broadcast, only seven on CBS, but that was judged sufficient. In addition, the network was having difficulty landing a regular sponsor. Naturally disappointed, Eastwood requested that the network let him out of his contract so he could appear in an episode of a show being produced at Fox and the film version of the Broadway hit *The Tall Story*. CBS said no, but director Arthur Lubin, a friend from his days at Universal, managed to talk the network into allowing Eastwood to play a town tough in an episode of *Maverick* ("Duel at Sundown") filmed at Warner Bros. and broadcast a few weeks after *Rawhide* debuted. Then, as he and his wife were riding on a train to Piedmont for Christmas, a telegram caught up to them: *Rawhide* was being scheduled on Friday nights as a midseason replacement for *The Jackie Gleason Show* and *Trackdown*, the Robert Culp series, which was shifted to Wednesday. Instrumental in this change of fortune was CBS founder William Paley, a big fan of Westerns who was enthusiastic about what he had seen of *Rawhide* and ordered the show onto the schedule, sponsored by Marlboro cigarettes.

In the beginning, Eastwood's acting skills were outpaced by those of the more experienced Fleming, Paul Brinegar and Sheb Wooley. Yet it was Eastwood, the young and handsome cowboy actor, whom *TV Guide* predictably chose to feature in its August 15, 1959, issue.

Clint Eastwood.

The article, entitled "How to Keep Fit," was accompanied by a color photograph of Eastwood, clad only in swimming trunks, doing pushups poolside. In addition to his tips on how to diet and exercise, the piece suggested "he could make a living as a stunt man, if necessary. On the *Rawhide* set he competes with stunt extras in Indian wrestling and in such tricks as holding a sledge upright in one hand at arm's length and letting the sledge down slowly toward his own head. Such horseplay is good for the series, Eastwood believes." Two years later, another Eastwood story in the magazine

Eric Fleming and Clint Eastwood.

was illustrated by a full page shot of him, shirtless, doing a handstand in front of some extras and crew members on the Western street at MGM.

In the same issue, he remarked, "We're doing stories as they pretty much happened. Oh, occasionally I guess we hoke one up for dramatic purposes, but generally speaking we're doing the kind of things that guys on the cattle drives really did."

Eastwood's acting rapidly improved as he became more comfortable with the character of Rowdy, and his interpretation of the role was often so effortless that he was sometimes accused of seeming bored. Director Ted Post, with whom Eastwood would later work in films (1968's *Hang 'em High*, 1973's *Magnum Force*) came to his defense, reminding critics that "Clint knows exactly what he's doing." Or as Eastwood put it, "Gary Cooper wasn't afraid to do nothing." (Cooper was famous for appearing uninvolved until a far different impression was projected on the screen.) "Having the security of being in a series, week in, week out, gives you great flexibility," Eastwood said. "You can experiment with yourself, try a different scene different ways. If you make a mistake one week, you can look at it and say, 'Well, I won't do that again,' and you're still on the air next week."

"*Rawhide* was a great training ground," he reflected in 1985. "All of a sudden everything you ever studied about being an actor you could put into play every day. In *Rawhide* I got to play every day. It taught me how to pick up and run, how to make things up, how to wing things in there."

He was also able to watch and learn from a broad cross section of aging film stars and character actors. "Every kind of person imaginable came through," he said. "That was a great experience for me, watching other people, seeing them operate, watching the different techniques." In a 1974 interview he observed, "In *Rawhide*, we had some sensational people—Julie Harris, Geraldine Page." Page co-starred with Eastwood in 1971's *The Beguiled*, but never guest starred on *Rawhide*.

Much the same as Michael Landon used the *Bonanza* set as a film school, Eastwood took advantage of his time on *Rawhide* to learn about everything from camera lenses and lighting effects to directing. "I just would watch everything," he said. "The old-timers, the new-timers and some of the hacks, too. You learn about leadership, how one week a crew can move very fast and efficiently and the next week drag. About ninety percent of the time it's the fault of the director." His request to be permitted to film a cattle stampede with a hand held camera was turned down by Warren on the grounds that he was not a member of the cinematographers union. Eastwood persisted, but was told by the network that actors who directed tended to go over budget and take too much time. Instead, Warren let him direct some promotional clips for the show, which was less than creatively satisfying.

Returning to his love of music, Eastwood, who sang in a few episodes of *Rawhide*, followed the current trend of television heartthrobs making records for mainly female fans. His first single, released in 1961, was "Unknown Girl of My Dreams," with "For All We Know" on the flipside. The next year he recorded "Rowdy," backed with "Cowboy Wedding Song." Both singles were on Cameo-Parkway, the same label that issued *Rawhide's Clint Eastwood Sings Cowboy Favorites*, a full length album, in 1963. In summer, Eastwood, Sheb Wooley and/or Paul Brinegar would tour the rodeo and state fair circuit, performing comedy sketches and musical numbers for as much as five thousand dollars apiece, substantially more than they were earning on the series. (In recent years, Clint has recorded with Merle Haggard, Ray Charles and Randy Travis.)

In March 1962, Eastwood made another appearance in *TV Guide*, this time for a photo feature about "some typical TV longhairs." Actors the magazine felt were in need of a barber included Bob Denver (*Dobie Gillis*), Chuck Connors (*The Rifleman*), Scott "Denny" Miller (*Wagon Train*) and Eastwood, who "insists that he has that flowing mane cut at least once a week, and that it isn't really long." In Eastwood's words, his hair was "course" and "what you might call a Western crew cut."

That same spring, CBS allowed Eastwood to appear in an episode of *Mr. Ed*, a formerly syndicated sitcom about a talking horse that the network had picked up the previous fall. The installment, co-written by Eastwood's friend Sonia Chernus, was entitled "Clint Eastwood Meets Mr. Ed" and intended to not only keep the increasingly restless actor happy but hopefully help *Rawhide's* sagging ratings.

At the beginning of the series' fourth season (1961-62), the character of Rowdy was finally fleshed out a bit more in an episode ("Rio Salado") where he meets up with his ne'er do well father. Whether this was done to placate Eastwood, or merely a creative decision on the part of Endre Bohem (who that year replaced Charles Marquis Warren as producer) is open to speculation. It is a fact, however, that under Bohem's guidance, the writers began to

Eastwood in *Fistful of Dollars* (1964).

place more emphasis on the regular cast.

By April 1964, CBS had loosened the contractual leash sufficiently so that Eastwood was able to take advantage of his first real opportunity to spread his creative wings beyond the show. He and buddy Bill Tompkins (drover Toothless on *Rawhide*) flew to Rome to appear in director Sergio Leone's *A Fistful of Dollars*, the first of three "Spaghetti Westerns" Eastwood would make with Leone. Eric Fleming was among the several television cowboys who had turned down the role of a mysterious gunfighter known as the Man with No Name, and both he and Richard Harrison, an actor specializing in Italian sword and sandal epics, recommended Eastwood. Leone screened an episode of *Rawhide* ("The Black Sheep") and, impressed by the actor's athleticism, offered the part to Eastwood, who also said no, but reconsidered after reading the script, which he recognized as a reworking of the classic Japanese film *Yojimbo*, directed by Akira Kurosawa (a fan of silent cowboy star William S. Hart) and released in 1961. Wearing much of his Rowdy garb and accessories, Eastwood made *Fistful*, then returned to Hollywood for a seventh

Eric Fleming and Clint Eastwood.

season of *Rawhide*, not learning until later that the film, not released in the United States until February 1967, was becoming a major hit in Europe, where it earned nearly five million dollars in three years. Eastwood was paid only fifteen thousand.

The *Rawhide* producers for the 1964-65 season decided Eastwood had not been used enough in previous years, and that at thirty-four he was too old to be playing Eric Fleming's young sidekick. Story editor Del Reisman, who had formerly worked on both *Playhouse 90* and *The Twilight Zone*, told Eastwood, "Don't get shocked. We're trying to mature the character." This did not sit well with Fleming, who usually did not need much of an excuse to complain about his dissatisfaction with the show. Nor did it please William Paley, a Fleming fan who in the past had warned *Rawhide* producers not to let Eastwood overshadow the older star. Paley also objected to the direction the show was taking. As a result, the new producers did not last the season. A tenuous balance between the Rowdy and Favor characters was somewhat restored, and *Rawhide* narrowly escaped cancellation.

In the spring of 1965, a year after agreeing to make his first film with Leone, Eastwood flew back to Rome to shoot the superior follow-up, *For a Few Dollars More*, which, like *Fistful of Dollars*, was based on a Kurosawa film (1962's *Sanjuro*, a sequel to *Yojimbo*) and not released domestically until 1967. This time, Eastwood's salary was increased to the considerably more fifty-thousand dollars. While there, he picked up a newspaper and was irritated to discover that not only had *Rawhide* been renewed for an eighth season, he was being promoted to trail boss. No one from CBS had bothered to tell him personally. The show's latest producer, Ben Brady, was dispatched to Rome to pacify Eastwood, who urged Brady to keep Fleming and let him go instead. Brady persisted, and Eastwood, who by now was making around $100,000 a year, reluctantly agreed to continue as Rowdy Yates. When a reporter asked him if he was happy about the renewal of the series, Eastwood replied, "Why should I be pleased? I used to carry half the shows. Now I carry them all. For the same money. CBS just said go to work. There was no talk about money or anything. In the first show of the season they don't even explain how Rowdy Yates is promoted from ramrod to trail boss."

During the final season, some aspects of Sergio Leone's Man with No Name creation seemed to merge with the character of Rowdy Yates. Eastwood played him as no longer boyish, seldom smiling and more than a little discontent. The evolution was interesting to watch, but it went on for only thirteen episodes. Had CBS followed through on its notion to shoot the series in color, or had it not unwisely scheduled it against the hugely popular *Combat!* on Tuesday night— a move that angered Eastwood—*Rawhide* may have at least been able to finish out the season.

It is largely because of *Rawhide* that Clint Eastwood is thought of as a Western hero, especially by older fans. (Younger people may understandably consider him "Dirty Harry.") Surprisingly, he has made only *ten* films that can be considered Westerns in the forty-five years since *Rawhide* left the air, and that includes such marginal entries as the musical *Paint Your Wagon* (1969) and the Civil War era film *The Beguiled* (1971). But the remaining eight, though some are better than others, are all worthy of repeated viewings.

The Good, the Bad, and the Ugly, the third and most epic in Sergio Leone's Man with No Name trilogy, was filmed in 1966, but not released until January 1968 in the United States, where it was a major hit despite suffering in comparison with *For a Few Dollars More*. Both Eastwood and co-star Lee Van Cleef (also in *For a Few Dollars More*) were frequently upstaged by Eli Wallach's colorful performance as Tuco, the Ugly of the title. Eastwood, who earned five times what he had been paid for the previous film, had no complaints. He did, however, turn down an offer to star in what would come to be viewed as Leone's masterpiece, 1969's *Once Upon a Time in the West*. The role instead went to Charles Bronson, who had been the Italian director's original choice for the Man with No Name five years before.

Hang 'em High (1968), directed by Eastwood's *Rawhide* associate Ted Post, was United Artists' attempt at a Spaghetti Western. It co-starred such *Rawhide* guest stars as Ed Begley, Pat Hingle, L.Q. Jones, Bruce Dern and Bob Steele.

Two Mules for Sister Sara (1970), co-starring Shirley MacLaine, found Eastwood portraying a character more similar to the Man with No Name than he had been in *Hang 'em High*, a trend that would continue more often than not.

The cast of *Joe Kidd* (1972) included Gregory Walcott and Dick Van Patten, who both appeared on *Rawhide*, but it was 1973's *High Plains Drifter*, directed by Eastwood himself, that earned the biggest smiles from *Rawhide* fans, for in the cast was none other than Paul "Wishbone" Brinegar. Similarly, *The Outlaw Josey Wales* (1976), also directed by Eastwood, featured another *Rawhide* reunion of sorts, with Sheb "Pete Nolan" Wooley as one of the supporting players.

Eastwood starred in, produced and directed *Pale Rider* (1985), in which his avenging hero was a combination of the Man with No Name and the title character from *Shane*. After that, he was involved in seven more films, none of them a Western, and he was frequently asked if he was ever going to do another. His response was always the same: If he found something he liked well enough.

That "something" turned out to be 1992's *Unforgiven*, which he again headlined, produced and directed. The latter duty earned him his first Academy Award as Best Director, and the film itself became only the third Western in movie history to be honored as Best Picture (the other two are *Cimarron* in 1931 and *Dances with Wolves* in 1990). Since then, Eastwood has been more interested in directing than acting, winning a second Oscar for helming 2004's *Million Dollar Baby*, also voted Best Picture.

In addition to the Irving G. Thalberg Memorial Award for lifetime achievement in film, he was given a Golden Boot Award in 1993.

A few years ago, an Internet rumor (started by a source impossible to verify) that Eastwood and Kevin Costner were going to take the Glenn Ford and Jack Lemmon roles in a remake of the 1958 film *Cowboy* was, like virtually all Internet rumors, untrue.

When asked by *TV Guide* in 1995 if he ever watches episodes of *Rawhide*, Eastwood replied, "I've got tapes of some episodes, and sometimes I see it when I'm channel surfing. The fact that nobody can remember the last Western series in prime time suggests to me that *Rawhide* and *Gunsmoke* and *Maverick* have withstood the test of time."

Indeed they have...

CHAPTER FOUR
THE GIL FAVOR OUTFIT

PAUL BRINEGAR
(GEORGE WASHINGTON WISHBONE, COOK)

One of only three major characters to remain with *Rawhide* for all eight seasons, audience favorite Paul Brinegar was also one of the busiest actors in Hollywood. Born on December 19, 1917, in Tucumcari, New Mexico, he began his acting career by participating in high school and college plays.

In the late 1940s he migrated to Hollywood and acted in small theater productions before landing his first film role, that of a gambler in, appropriately, the 1946 Western *Abilene Town*, starring Randolph Scott. Coincidentally, Abilene would be one of the major destinations of the Gil Favor outfit on *Rawhide*. Before the decade was over, Brinegar managed to obtain bit parts in such films as *Larceny* (1948), *Take One False Step* (1949), *Sword in the Desert* (1949) and *The Gal Who Took the West* (1949), not always receiving onscreen credit.

The trend of seldom being billed continued for the next five years, but Brinegar was rarely unemployed, appearing in more than twenty films (including the Westerns *A Ticket to Tomahawk*, *Rails into Laramie* and *Four Guns to the Border*) and on such television series as *Racket Squad*, *Ford Theatre*, *The Public Defender*, *The Loretta Young Show*, *Fireside Theatre* and "Rendezvous at Whipsaw," an episode of *The Lone Ranger*.

When the second season of *The Life and Times of Wyatt Earp* debuted in 1956, Brinegar had been added to the cast as Mayor Jim "Dog" Kelly, his first steady job. He continued with the series through its third season, all the while being permitted to accept

Brinegar and unknown.

work in films and on other shows, including *Tales of the Texas Rangers, Whirlybirds, The Adventures of Jim Bowie* and *Cheyenne.* In an episode of the latter, "Lone Gun," Hal Baylor, one of Brinegar's future *Rawhide* co-stars, played a character coincidentally known as Rowdy.

During 1957, Brinegar remained active, appearing in episodes of *Alfred Hitchcock Presents, The 20th Century-Fox Hour, Sugarfoot* and an episode of *Tales of Wells Fargo* ("Renegade Raiders") whose guest cast included Western icons Dan Blocker, Denver Pyle and Morgan Woodward. Of the three films he made that year—*The Vampire, Hell on Devil's Island* and *Copper Sky*—it was the third that had the most significance, teaming Brinegar with the picture's executive producer, Charles Marquis Warren.

In 1958's *Cattle Empire*, produced and directed by Warren, Brinegar was cast as the drive's cook, Thomas Jefferson Jeffrey, who reveals that his brother's name is George Washington Jeffrey. Co-writer Endre Bohem was evidently taken with brothers' names—the cook on *Rawhide* was dubbed George Washington Wishbone, and in one episode he meets up with his brother, Thomas Jefferson Wishbone.

Brinegar, however, was not the first actor to portray Wishbone. In the original, unaired pilot of the series, Robert Carricart was cast as the drive's Mexican cook. Carricart was no stranger to the television prairie, having done several shows, including four episodes of *Have Gun-Will Travel*. But, as Brinegar recalled, "For some reason or other, the studio didn't feel the Mexican cook was working out very well. Warren remembered me and brought me in. So I spent seven happy years as Wishbone, having a ball with all of the guys, traveling the country making personal appearances. When we'd go out on personal appearances, Sheb would always have Clint or I do the funny little noises he'd done himself on the record ("The Purple People Eater"). We both screwed it up."

While CBS debated what to do about putting *Rawhide* on the prime time schedule, Brinegar wasted no time going after other jobs, making episodes of *Lawman*, *The Texan*, *Trackdown* and another *Sugarfoot*.

More than a few of Brinegar's co-workers maintain that he could be just as cranky as Wishbone, yet he beamed as brightly as a kid on Christmas morning when introduced by Eric Fleming on a segment of the game show *Stump the Stars*. "Here's Wishbone!" Fleming announced to the accompaniment of thundering audience applause. "Everybody knows Wishbone!"

On *Rawhide*, Brinegar stole virtually every scene he was in, whether shouting at Mushy, his not-very-bright assistant, or displaying the more tender side of his nature when the drive crossed paths with members of the opposite sex. No mere second banana, Wishbone, revealed to be a former mountain man, was often the central character in many of the show's more memorable episodes, including "Incident of the Tinker's Dam," "Incident of the Deserter," "Incident of the Rusty Shotgun," "Incident of the Pied Piper" and "Mrs. Harmon."

Paul Brinegar and Eastwood.

When the characters of Gil Favor and Mushy—Wishbone's partner in comic antics—were eliminated prior to the start of *Rawhide's* final season, Brinegar angrily told the press that he was in "utter shock." The network, he said, had "decimated the cast." Before the series was canceled, he and new regular Raymond St. Jacques agreed that *Rawhide's* future prospects did not look good.

After the show folded, Brinegar was not idle for long, embarking once again on a long career of varied character roles on non-Western series from *Cannon, Emergency, CHiPs, Knight Rider, Medical Center,* the new version of *Perry Mason, Petrocelli, The Dukes of Hazzard, The Six Million Dollar Man* and *Trapper John, M.D.* to the frontier tales *Daniel Boone, Bonanza, The Life and Times of Grizzly Adams, The Guns of Will Sonnett, The Iron Horse, The Barbary Coast* and *Little House on the Prairie.* He also found regular employment as Jelly Hoskins on the second season (1969-70) of *Lancer,* the first season (1982-83) of *Matt Houston* and, in 1986, the daytime soap opera *Capitol.*

In 1969 he was reunited with former *Rawhide* co-star Charles Gray in Elvis Presley's *Charro,* co-written and directed by none other than Charles Marquis Warren. Four years later, he appeared in Clint Eastwood's *High Plains Drifter,* followed by *The Creature Wasn't Nice, Chattanooga Choo Choo* and the Mel Brooks comedy *Life Stinks.*

Never officially retiring, Brinegar was working as late as 1994, humorously playing a stagecoach driver in the big screen resurrection of *Maverick,* starring Mel Gibson and James Garner. Prior to that, he was cast as the same character in two episodes of the short-lived Western series *The Adventures of Brisco County, Jr.* Although brief, he made an amusing cameo appearance as a trail drive cook ("Cookie," a name Wishbone resented being called) in *The Luck of the Draw,* the fourth Kenny Rogers "Gambler" film for television. In an imaginative monologue, Cookie manages to work in the name of several vintage TV Westerns, including, of course, *Rawhide.*

Paul Brinegar was honored with a Golden Boot Award in 1994. Just as fond of pipe tobacco as his *Rawhide* character, he succumbed to emphysema at the age of seventy-seven in Los Angeles on March 27, 1995.

RIGHT AND BELOW:
Eastwood, Brinegar and Fleming.

SHEB WOOLEY
(PETE NOLAN, SCOUT)

Sheb Wooley looked like either a country singer or a cowboy. He was both. Born in Erick, Oklahoma, on April 10, 1921, he was enamored of music from an early age, learning guitar and forming his own band by the age of fifteen. Known as the Plainview Melody Boys, they managed to secure their own show on a radio station in Elk City, located some thirty miles northeast of Erick.

Nine years later, in 1945, Wooley decided to head down to Nashville and break into the music business as a singer and songwriter. No less a country icon than Ernest Tubb felt that he had talent, yet getting noticed among hundreds of aspiring country hopefuls in Music City proved difficult. Wooley managed to record four of his compositions for Bullet Records, two of which were never released and two that sat on the shelf for more than a few years. Undaunted, he began performing wherever he could around the Nashville area, his persistence resulting in being given two regular spots on radio station WLAC.

In 1947, encouraged by the top executive of a major music publishing firm, Wooley decided to hit Hollywood and try his luck as a singing cowboy in the mold of Gene Autry and Roy Rogers. Instead, he wound up in Fort Worth, Texas, where he not only snagged his own radio program but formed a band, the Calumet Indians, its name taken from the show's sponsor, Calumet Baking Powder.

Wooley finally made it to Hollywood by 1950 and, like Paul Brinegar, began appearing in small theater productions around town. A talent scout for Warner Bros. happened to be in the audience of one play and asked him if he would be interested in doing a screen test for an Errol Flynn Western. Stunned, Wooley did not hesitate to accept the offer. Soon after, he was on location in New Mexico to shoot *Rocky Mountain*, a Civil War era film in which soldiers from the Union and the Confederacy team up to battle Indians. Other cast members included such Western veterans as Guinn "Big Boy" Williams, Dick Jones, Chubby Johnson and the legendary stunt man Yakima Canutt. Besides Wooley, another actor making his celluloid debut was Louis Lindley, better known as Slim Pickens.

Following that auspicious beginning, Wooley received no on screen credit in three of the four films he made during 1951: *Apache Drums, Inside the Walls of Folsom Prison* and *Distant Drums*, the latter starring Gary Cooper. An exception was director Charles Marquis Warren's *Little Big Horn*, in which Wooley portrayed a cavalry trooper named Quince, later the name given to actor Steve Raines' character on *Rawhide*.

Wooley made his first appearances on television in 1952, cast in two episodes of *The Cisco Kid* and four episodes of the syndicated Jock Mahoney series *The Range Rider* that did not air until the following year. But it was on the big screen that he remained busiest. He sang on film for the first time in the Las Vegas "Western" *Sky Full of Moon*, played a gambler in the modern Robert Mitchum Western *The Lusty Men*, and found himself back in the Old West for *Bugles in the Afternoon, Cattle Town, The Toughest Man in Tombstone*, Warren's *Hellgate* and, most prominently, as outlaw Frank Miller's brother Ben in the Gary Cooper classic *High Noon*.

The next year was comparatively lean, with Wooley making only one film, *Texas Badman*, doing two episodes of *The Adventures of Kit Carson*, two of *The Lone Ranger*, and not accomplishing much in the way of songwriting.

However, 1954 was a huge improvement on both creative fronts. Singers Theresa Brewer and Hank Snow each had hit records with Sheb Wooley compositions, and acting jobs once again began piling up. He made five films, including *The Boy from Oklahoma* (on which the TV series *Sugarfoot* was based), *Arrow in the Dust*, and the rather offbeat Joan Crawford Western *Johnny Guitar*. On the home screen he appeared in more episodes of *The Adventures of Kit Carson* and *The Lone Ranger*, and portrayed outlaw Jim Younger on *Stories of the Century*.

Wooley had the chance to work with Kirk Douglas, Richard Boone, Claire Trevor and Jay C. Flippen in director King Vidor's 1955 film *Man without a Star*. That same year he added to his growing list of television credits by doing yet more episodes of *The Lone Ranger* and *The Adventures of Kit Carson* as well as an episode of *The Adventures of Rin Tin Tin*.

Wooley worked for Charles Marquis Warren twice in 1956, first in *The Black Whip*, their third film together, and then in the unsold pilot for the proposed series *Cavalry Patrol*, whose cast included Charles Gray, later Wooley's replacement on *Rawhide*. Elsewhere, he was in episodes of *My Friend Flicka* and *Dick Powell's Zane Grey Theatre*, the theatrical feature *The Oklahoman*, and, most important, the James Dean classic *Giant*.

During 1957, a full third of the Top Thirty shows on television in the year-end ratings were Westerns: *Gunsmoke, Tales of Wells Fargo, Have Gun Will Travel, The Life and Legend of Wyatt Earp, The Restless Gun, Cheyenne, Dick Powell's Zane Grey Theatre, Wagon Train, Sugarfoot* and *Zorro*. Wooley had guest roles on four of them (*Cheyenne, Sugarfoot, Tales of Wells Fargo* and *Wyatt Earp*) and did episodes of *Trackdown* and *Maverick* and *Ford Television Theatre*. He also teamed up with director Warren once again for two films, *Trooper Hook* and *Ride a Violent Mile*.

Even after all this activity, Wooley received no screen credit for 1958's *Terror in a Texas Town*, but his days of occasional anonymity were about to change. "I landed *Rawhide* because I'd done a couple of pictures for Charles Marquis Warren," he said. He had, of course, actually made five films for Warren, who reportedly had only Wooley in mind when it came time to cast trail drive scout Pete Nolan.

The Nolan character was essential to the series, responsible for finding water, good grass, locating the best place for the herd to ford a river, looking for signs of trouble, seeing if the next town had a doctor, and more. Even so, Wooley was not given a story almost entirely his own until "Incident of the Roman Candles," the last episode of the first season, wherein he demonstrated his ability to be more than a supporting player. For the next few years there would be at least one Pete Nolan showcase per season, with Wooley's presence expanded in several others, particularly "Incident of the Dust Flower," "Incident of the Slavemaster," "Incident of the Fish Out of Water," "Incident of the New Start" and "Incident of His Brother's Keeper."

Wooley was occasionally written out of episodes so that he could concentrate on his music career, which had suddenly caught fire just as the first episodes of *Rawhide* went into production. "Purple People Eater," a novelty song he came up with to cash in on the public's current obsession with UFOs (and which MGM Records

Eastwood, Fleming and Sheb Wooley.

originally did not want to release), was a smash, spending most of June and July 1958 at the top of Billboard's list of weekly hits. According to *Cash Box* magazine, Wooley's record, which he wrote under the alias Ben Colder, sold over one million copies in less than a month and was the number thirteen seller of the year.

During *Rawhide*'s third season, Wooley co-wrote the story on which the script for "Incident of the Blackstorms" was based. It aired in May 1961, roughly the same time Charles Marquis Warren was preparing to hand the reins of the series over to Endre Bohem—and when Wooley announced that he wanted to leave sometime during the upcoming season to resume his music activities full-time.

The eventual replacement, a drover of dubious repute by the name of Clay Forrester, was introduced in "Inside Man," the sixth episode of season four. Forrester was played by Charles Gray, who had been in Warren's *Cattle Empire* as well as two early episodes of *Rawhide* as different characters. He disappeared for the next five episodes before officially joining the series. After another five episodes, Wooley seemed to be gone for good, only to reappear eight weeks later in an episode appropriately entitled "Reunion." That same year, 1962, he scored a number one country hit, "That's My Pa."

At least one tabloid of the era hinted, falsely, that Wooley left the show due to a salary dispute. Another suggested that he was jealous of Eastwood's larger role, also false. "Clint and I partied quite a bit," Wooley recalled. "Wishbone didn't party with us, nor did Eric. Clint and I partied everywhere we went! That's what we did best. Neither one of us could act, but we *could* party."

When *Rawhide* was stumbling badly in its seventh season, both creatively and in the ratings, Wooley was asked to return for several episodes in an effort to rekindle the show's original spark. On February 5, 1965, viewers tuned in and were no doubt pleasantly surprised to see Pete Nolan back with the drive, even if he was about to be hanged for murder. CBS announced that Wooley would be returning to the series on a regular basis for the eighth season, but producer Ben Brady decided otherwise, saying it would be too expensive to bring him back.

Wooley, managed by his wife Linda, continued to be a success in the musical entertainment field, winning the Country Music Association's Comedian of the Year award in 1968. The next year he wrote the theme for the CBS country music variety series *Hee Haw*, appeared in the first thirteen installments, and continued to do occasional guest shots. He also guest starred in episodes of *The Mod Squad* in 1969 and *The Young Rebels* in 1970, his last television work for nearly fifteen years.

In 1976, Wooley and Clint Eastwood were reunited in the latter's *The Outlaw Josey Wales*, the first film—and Western—Wooley had made since John Wayne's *The War Wagon* nine years earlier. He did no more acting until the Jane Fonda television movie *The Dollmaker*, in 1984, followed the next year by the big budget *Silverado*, his final role in a Western.

Wooley's last three films were *Uphill All the Way* and *Hoosiers*, both 1986, and *Purple People Eater* (based, of course, on his hit record) in 1988. His swan song was a role on television's *Murder, She Wrote*, in 1990.

Sheb Wooley died in Nashville on September 16, 2003, a victim of leukemia. His funeral service began at high noon, his casket covered by the saddle blanket he had used in his first film, *Rocky Mountain*.

STEVE RAINES
(JIM QUINCE, DROVER AND RAMROD)

Steve Raines, though short and wiry, had the advantage of looking and sounding as if he actually could have been a cattle drover. Born on June 17, 1916, he was both a stunt man and character actor long before becoming one of only three regulars to remain on *Rawhide* for its entire run. Starting in the late 1940s, he worked most often as a member of an outlaw gang on such nearly forgotten B Westerns as *Along the Oregon Trail, Under Colorado Skies, Oklahoma Badlands, Frontier Revenge, Sheriff of Wichita, Son of a Badman, Border Fence* and *Drums Across the River.*

Raines' first major film was the 1953 Alan Ladd classic *Shane*, after which he soon found regular employment on the television range. Between 1954 and 1956 he became a familiar face on episodes of *The Adventures of Kit Carson, The Gene Autry Show, Brave Eagle* and *The Roy Rogers Show.* He also appeared in two feature films, Columbia's *Count Three and Pray* and the independently produced *The Naked Gun.*

Certainly his most important job, albeit minor in terms of screen time, was Charles Marquis Warren's *Cattle Empire*, which led directly to his being cast as *Rawhide's* Jim Quince. While doing the show, he was permitted to take outside work, including episodes of *The Life and Legend of Wyatt Earp* and *The Tall Man*, both in 1961.

A better actor than his fellow drover Rocky Shahan, Raines was frequently given equally as much to do as Sheb Wooley. In 1960, he and a friend submitted a script called "Incident at Rojo Canyon," the first episode of the third season. The next year, Jim Quince was finally given his own episode, "Judgment at Hondo Seco," which found Raines holding his own among a strong guest cast that included Ralph Bellamy, Roy Barcroft and Ray Teal.

For *Rawhide*'s ill-fated final season, Quince was promoted to ramrod after producer Ben Brady scuttled plans to bring back Sheb Wooley's Pete Nolan. Raines, Brady reasoned, was cheaper. Raines' status as one of the few remaining members of the original cast did not necessarily guarantee more exposure for Jim Quince, who was allowed a large share of the spotlight for only one of the last thirteen episodes, "Walk into Terror." Shortly before the series was canceled, Raines complained publicly that he was not impressed with the quality of the scripts he was seeing, but it was far too late to remedy the situation.

For the next nine years, Raines was active mainly on television, seen in *The Iron Horse, Laredo, Daniel Boone, Walt Disney, Bonanza, The Guns of Will Sonnett, The Virginian, The Wild Wild West, The High Chaparral* and more than a dozen episodes of *Gunsmoke*. It was on the latter that he gave his final appearance, in the 1974 episode "The Tarnished Badge." His sole feature credit during this period was 1970's *Macho Callahan*, a Civil War era film directed by one-time *Rawhide* producer Bernard Kowalski.

Steve Raines suffered a stroke and died in Grants Pass, Oregon, on January 4, 1996, less than six months before his eightieth birthday.

JAMES MURDOCK
(HARKNESS "MUSHY" MUSHGROVE III)

Paul Brinegar was once overheard telling a fan that there was not much difference between Mushy—*Rawhide*'s dimwitted "cook's louse"—and James Murdock, the young actor who portrayed him. According to others, including multiple guest star Gregory Walcott, Murdock was simply a quiet, somewhat awkward, yet likeable young man. If one watches the earliest episodes carefully, Mushy, Wishbone's culinary assistant for seven seasons, is not the bumbling bumpkin he was soon to become, evidently to provide the series with occasional comic relief. According to Charles Gray, Mushy was the favorite character of screen legend Paul Muni.

Murdock was born in Illinois on June 22, 1931, and there is no public record of what he did between then and showing up as an extra with only two brief scenes in a 1958 episode of *Trackdown*. A few months later, he had a few lines of dialogue on *Have Gun-Will Travel*.

Like most members of the Gil Favor outfit, Mushy was a former Confederate soldier, and the only one who still wore his soldier's cap. His naïve outlook on life, as well as his desire to graduate from Wishbone's flunky to full fledged drover, provided the basis for several humorous and even poignant episodes. For the third season's "Incident of the Captive," in which Mushy's mother catches up to the drive and asks him to quit, Murdock, rather than Eric Fleming, had the opportunity to recite the opening narration. Several weeks later, in "Incident of the Big Blowout," Mushy was given a love interest in the person of a young school teacher. The following season, in "The Child Woman," viewers were introduced to Mushy's cousin.

During *Rawhide*'s erratic seventh season, Murdock figured prominently in two of the better episodes, particularly "A Man Called Mushy," written by soon-to-be *Gunsmoke* producer John Mantley. Coincidentally, the other episode, "El Hombre Bravo," was both written and directed by *Gunsmoke* veterans, Herman Groves and Philip Leacock, respectively. "El Hombre Bravo" featured the unusual pairing of Mushy and Gil Favor. In Murdock's last appearance on *Rawhide*, "The Gray Rock Hotel," he was given a rare opportunity to portray Mushy as something other than a buffoon.

Eliminated from the cast prior to the eighth season, Murdock had little luck furthering his career. In 1965 he did an episode of *The Chrysler Theatre*, Bob Hope's NBC anthology program, followed by guest shots on the first episode of ABC's Western series *The Monroes* and an episode of *Gunsmoke*, both in 1966. They were, as near as can be determined, his final acting jobs.

James Murdock died of pneumonia in Los Angeles on Christmas Eve, 1981. He was 50 years of age.

ROCKY SHAHAN
(JOE SCARLETT, DROVER)

With a stern countenance that disguised an easygoing and even mischievous nature, Joe Scarlett, as portrayed by former stunt man and wrangler Rocky Shahan, was one of *Rawhide*'s more authentic assets. He never said much, nor did the writers give him much to do, but that did not matter. The mere sight of barrel-chested Shahan, either galloping alongside the herd or simply sitting around the campfire, was enough to almost make viewers believe they were witnessing scenes from the nineteenth century. On those infrequent occasions when he spoke, pulled a gag or sprang into action, Scarlett was definitely noticed.

Shahan tended to maintain and low profile, and, like James Murdock, not much is known about him. He started his Hollywood career in the late 1940s, playing bit parts and performing stunts or doubling actors in serials and such features as *Across the Wide Missouri, The Lusty Men, Wyoming Roundup, Johnny Guitar, The Storm Rider, Run for Cover, The Jubilee Trail, The Deerslayer* and 1957's *Copper Sky*, whose cast included Paul Brinegar.

On the small screen he worked as either an extra, a stunt man, or both, on *The Range Rider, Tales of the Texas Rangers, Have Gun-Will Travel* and *Stories of the Century*. Like several other *Rawhide* regulars, he also worked on Charles Marquis Warren's *Cattle Empire*.

When producers Bruce Geller and Bernard Kowalski took over the running of *Rawhide* for the seventh season, they made the unfortunate decision to drop two longtime characters—wrangler Hey-Soos and drover Joe Scarlett. They were, however, brought back briefly toward the end of the season, when Geller and Kowalski were relieved of their duties.

Rocky Shahan, whose last documented appearance was as a stage-coach driver in the 1964 *Gunsmoke* episode "Jonah Hutchinson," died on December 8, 1981.

Robert Cabal (bottom row, 3rd from left), Sheb Wooley (3rd row, left), Clint Eastwood (3rd row, third from left) join cast members and guest stars from *Laramie*, *Gunsmoke*, *Wagon Train* and *Tales of Wells Fargo* (1961).

ROBERT CABAL
(HEY-SOOS PATINES, WRANGLER)

Yet another *Rawhide* regular with an enigmatic background was Robert Cabal, about whom not much is known. Appropriately, his character, superstitious horse wrangler Hey-Soos—apparently someone connected with the show or at CBS was uncomfortable listing someone named Jesus in the cast—could usually be relied on to be on hand whenever the drive encountered unexplained phenomenon or mysterious strangers.

His earliest screen work dates from the late 1940s to the mid-1950s, when he was often uncredited in the films *Ride the Pink Horse*, *The Saxon Charm*, *The Bribe*, *Border Incident*, *Forbidden Jungle*, *Crisis*, *Maru Maru* and *Escape to Burma*, *Hell's Island*, *Jungle Hell*, *Around the World in Eighty Days*, and his first Western, 1953's *The Man Behind the Gun*, starring Randolph Scott.

On television he worked mainly in Westerns, landing roles on *The Cisco Kid, Hopalong Cassidy, Annie Oakley, Broken Arrow, The Californians* and *Have Gun-Will Travel*. Even after joining *Rawhide*, he made episodes of *The Life and Legend of Wyatt Earp* and *Stagecoach West*. This is understandable considering how long it took *Rawhide* producer Charles Marquis Warren to decide if Hey-Soos was going to be a regular cast member.

Not introduced until the eighteenth episode, "Incident Below the Brazos," in which Cabal was listed among the guest stars, Hey-Soos disappeared for the remainder of the season. When Cabal was seen again, it was in the second season's "Incident of the Day of the Dead," wherein he played not Hey-Soos, but a ranch hand. Hey-Soos did not return until "Incident of the Blue Fire," episode thirty-three, and Cabal was again listed among the guest stars. Several weeks later, in "Incident at Sulphur Creek" and "Incident of the Dancing Death," Hey-Soos was back, but it was not until the back-to-back episodes "Incident of the One Hundred Amulets" and "Incident of the Murder Steer" toward the end of the second season that it seemed as if he might become more than a semi-regular. In fact, the first of the two episodes included Hey-Soos' mother.

When the third season began, Hey-Soos was in the second episode, "Incident of the Challenge," but Cabal was still credited as a guest star, a trend that continued each time he appeared until his name was included with the rest of the regulars in the final two episodes of the season. Oddly, Hey-Soos was absent in both.

Along with Rocky Shahan, Cabal was dropped from *Rawhide* in 1964, only to come back for a handful of episodes in early 1965. Later that year, he had a small role in an episode of *The Big Valley* before evidently abandoning his acting career.

Late in 2004, the Screen Actors Guild revealed that Robert Cabal had passed away more than a year before, on May 11, 2003, age and cause of death unknown.

CHARLES GRAY
(CLAY FORRESTER, SCOUT)

Charles Gray, born in Omaha, Nebraska, in 1922, was by far the most highly educated member of the *Rawhide* ensemble. Prior to the start of his acting career, he taught at both Tulane and the University of Houston, becoming so interested in theater that he established one of his own in Houston. When producer Sam Katzman came to town to shoot location footage for *The Houston Story*, a contemporary drama starring Gene Barry (television's *Bat Masterson*), Gary auditioned and was awarded with a small part. By the time the film was eventually released, in 1956, he had moved to Hollywood and made *One Desire*, starring Anne Baxter and Rock Hudson.

Gray's long association with producer/director Charles Marquis Warren began with the unsold 1956 pilot *Cavalry Patrol*, followed by seven Warren films in a row: *Tension at Table Rock*, *The Black Whip*, *Trooper Hook*, *Ride a Violent Mile*, *The Unknown Terror*, *Desert Hell* and, most momentous, 1958's *Cattle Empire*. On television, aside from an episode of *Highway Patrol*, he worked exclusively in Westerns, including three guest roles on *Gunsmoke*, two on *Zane Grey Theatre*, *Black Saddle*, *The Texan*, *Yancey Derringer*, *Have Gun-Will Travel*, *Death Valley Days*, *Riverboat* and two early episodes of *Rawhide* ("Incident of the Golden Calf," "Incident of the Haunted Hills"). Fortuitously, he had learned how to ride a horse as young boy.

During the late 1950s and very early 1960s, television was filled with several interesting yet short-lived Western series, *Hotel De Paree*, *The Westerner*, *Whispering Smith*, *Tate*, *Wrangler* and *Wichita Town* among them. Another was the hour long *Gunslinger*, Charles Marquis Warren's first project after exiting *Rawhide* in 1961, with a title song performed by Frankie Laine, vocalist of the *Rawhide* theme. The series was Gray's first regular acting job, billed third—as Pico McGuire—after stars Tony Young and Preston Foster. *Gunslinger* took over the Thursday night time slot of *The Witness*, a canceled legal drama, but only thirteen episodes were broadcast by CBS between February and September. Before the final installment aired, Gray had signed on as Clay Forrester for *Rawhide's* fourth season. "I didn't want to join an established family," he said, "and I already knew the chemistry was set on the show. I thought I'd get lost—and I did—but they made it attractive, so I joined."

Depending on one's perception, Forrester was either a bold, upstanding cattleman or a sinister gunman out to rustle a cattleman's stock. This ambiguous quality gave the character an intriguing edge, particularly in his first episode ("The Inside Man"), where he was revealed to be working for a man intent on stealing Gil Favor's herd. "I wanted to play him as an Aussie," Gray said, "which would have made it distinctive and fun for me, but I couldn't sell it to them. So the writers, Endre Bohem and I decided to make him just a little off the wall, a little suspect, looking for the main advantage, but actually a man loyal to those he called his friends." Nothing more was seen of Forrester for five weeks, and because the network wanted a certain episode for the holidays ("Twenty-Five Santa Clauses," aired on December 22, 1961), he was shown as being one of Favor's men a week before the story ("The Long Count") in which he was officially hired. After five more episodes, Sheb Wooley was gone (though he returned once before the season was over), and Gray took over as the drive's scout in "The Greedy Town." "It wasn't long before I discovered I was really just insurance, a built-in replacement, if the boys acted up or threatened to leave. Not a nice spot."

When *Rawhide* returned for its fifth season in September 1962, Gray figured prominently in the first episode, "Incident of the Hunter." Gregory Walcott, making the third of his five guest appearances on the series, remembered him as "a leading man type." Gray was unmistakably comfortable in his character's skin, confident enough to become the third member of the cast to contribute a story, "Incident of the Married Widow." Although written for Clay Forrester, the producers instead substituted Gil Favor, to Gray's understandable disappointment. "I decided to leave gracefully," Gray said, "and I did." The episode was broadcast on March 1, 1963. Viewers saw the last of Clay Forrester shortly after, on March 29, in "Incident of the Clown." By the last episode of the season, five weeks later, Jim Quince had been promoted to scout, with no mention of what had happened to Forrester. "I look with fondness on those days," Gray recalled, "because at the time I was also running a theater that I founded, so I was not locked into performing only one role, I kept busy."

Curiously, Clay was seen one last time, more than a year later, when "Incident of El Toro," an episode held over from 1962, was shown on April 9, 1964, leading many sources to conclude that Gray stayed with the series longer than he actually did. "I'm not sure I was ever aware of that," he remarked shortly before his death. "I was doing a lot of other things by then."

Those "other things" were episodes of *Hallmark Hall of Fame, Laredo, The Road West, The Iron Horse, Alias Smith & Jones, Bonanza, The High Chaparral, Gunsmoke,* and the made-for-television movie *This Savage Land,* co-starring Barry Sullivan, Glenn Corbett and George C. Scott, in 1969. The same year, he was reunited with writer/director Charles Marquis Warren for the Elvis Presley Western *Charro!,* whose cast also happened to include Paul Brinegar. Gray's last performances were in Steve McQueen's *Junior Bonner* (1972) and the 1978 television film *A Love Affair: The Eleanor and Lou Gehrig Story.*

Charles Gray was always courteous toward fans, corresponding via letters and in the pages of *Western Clippings,* edited and published by Boyd Magers. Gray maintained homes in Joshua Tree, California, and Center Sandwich, New Hampshire, where he died of a heart attack on August 2, 2008.

JOHN IRELAND
(JED COLBY, SCOUT)

John Ireland was doubtlessly the most experienced actor to join the cast of *Rawhide,* as well as the only one with an Academy Award nomination on his resume. Regrettably, his time with the series was brief.

Ireland was born in Vancouver, British Columbia, on January 30, 1914, and had performed Shakespeare on Broadway before migrating to Hollywood sometime during the 1940s. His first screen appearance was in the 1945 World War II classic *A Walk in the Sun.* Four years later, he was up for the Best Supporting Actor Oscar in *All the King's Men,* but lost to *Twelve O'Clock High*'s Dean Jagger.

Before his death at the age of the seventy-eight, his film and television credits numbered well over 200, many of them in Westerns.

John Ireland.

During the 1940s he was in *My Darling Clementine*, *I Shot Jesse James*, *Roughshod*, *The Doolins of Oklahoma* and *Red River*, one of the inspirations for *Rawhide*. In the 1950s he was seen in *The Return of Jesse James*, *Vengeance Valley*, *Red Mountain*, *The Bushwhackers*, *Southwest Passage*, *Gunslinger* and *Gunfight at the O.K. Corral*. He also starred in Charles Marquis Warren's *Little Big Horn*, and both co-starred and directed 1953's *Outlaw Territory*, originally entitled *Hannah Lee*. On television, he made some Western-themed installments of the anthology series *Schlitz Playhouse of the Stars* as well as episodes of *Zane Grey Theatre* and *Riverboat*.

For the first half of the 1960s, he worked mainly on television but guest starred on only such contemporary series as *Kraft Suspense Theatre*, *Alfred Hitchcock Presents* and *Burke's Law*, with one exception— three episodes of *Rawhide*, the first, "Incident in the Garden of Eden," at the end of the second season. He returned in the third season for "Incident of the Portrait," one of the best episodes of the entire series, and finally 1965's "The Spanish Camp," broadcast less than six months before he joined the cast.

Ireland was not immediately hired as Jed Colby for the final season, but after the top brass at CBS got a look at the first four episodes that had been filmed, it was determined that something was missing. That "something" was a well-known actor, preferably someone a bit older than Clint Eastwood who could at least partially fill the void left by Eric Fleming. A big name co-star would also give Eastwood some needed time off rather than requiring him to be in every episode. Executive producer Ben Brady chose Ireland, saying that the veteran actor "will give us recognizable value. He will add dramatic strength. He will play what is obviously a man his own age—touching forty." In truth, Ireland was approaching fifty-one.

Although it was actually the fifth episode to be filmed, trail scout Jed Colby was introduced in the second one of the season, "Ride a Crooked Mile." Typical of television in that era, there was no explanation as to where he came from, just as viewers were never told what happened to Gil Favor. As the network hoped, Ireland's character did have an air of world-weary authority. Unfortunately, the only storyline he had to himself, "The Vasquez Woman," was perhaps the weakest of the season.

After *Rawhide*, Ireland continued working until the end of his life, making films both foreign and domestic, co-starring with Angie Dickinson in the short-lived detective show *Cassie & Company*, and taking guest roles on numerous television series, including such Westerns as *A Man Called Shenandoah*, *Branded*, *The Iron Horse*, *Bonanza*, *Daniel Boone*, *Gunsmoke*, *The Men from Shiloh*, *The Quest*, *Little House on the Prairie* and the 1988 television movie *Bonanza:*

The Next Generation. The following year, he was honored with a Golden Boot Award.

John Ireland's last appearance was portraying King Arthur in the low-budget horror sequel *Waxwork II: Lost in Time*, released in 1992, the same year he died of leukemia in Santa Barbara, California, on March 21.

RAYMOND ST. JACQUES
(SIMON BLAKE, DROVER)

The first two black actors to be cast as regular characters on a television drama made their debuts one night apart, in September 1965. Although *I Spy*'s Bill Cosby is mentioned most often when this historic development is discussed, Raymond St. Jacques was introduced as *Rawhide*'s Simon Blake the previous evening.

St. Jacques was born James Arthur Johnson in Hartford, Connecticut, on March 1, 1930. Bitten early by the proverbial acting bug, he began writing and performing one act plays in grade school. Nearly twenty-five years later, after military service in Korea, he settled in New York, where he auditioned successfully for the prestigious Actor's Studio. At first he used the stage name Raymond Johnson, but had changed it by the time he had joined the American Shakespearean Festival in Stratford, Connecticut. He acquired skills in directing and fencing before his first Broadway show, the 1955 musical production *Seventh Heaven*. The following year, he made his initial filmed appearance in an episode of the NBC anthology series *Producer's Showcase*. He returned to the stage, seven years passing until again stepping in front of a camera, this time for an episode of the CBS medical drama *East Side/West Side*, starring George C. Scott.

Beginning with the groundbreaking *Black Like Me* (1964), St. Jacques found himself working primarily in film and on television. After episodes of *Slattery's People, Dr. Kildare* and *The Defenders*, he was cast in director Sidney Lumet's 1965 classic *The Pawnbroker* and the lesser *Mister Moses*, starring Robert Mitchum.

Tall, athletic and experienced, St. Jacques was the logical choice when *Rawhide* producer Ben Brady went looking for the first major black cowboy in television's version of the Old West. "St. Jacques is not being brought in because it is sociologically opportune to have a Negro in a sympathetic role, or to placate civil rights groups," Brady told a reporter. "St. Jacques will be a drover, exactly the same way as any white drover, except he's colored. There will be no reference to race."

Needless to say, St. Jacques was an interesting addition to the series, but few of the eighth season's thirteen episodes showcased his thespian skills or his character's appeal.

Although he continued working until the end of his life, St. Jacques rarely revisited the wild frontier, guest starring on only *The Virginian, Daniel Boone* and *Little House on the Prairie* in the dozen years following *Rawhide*.

He received the Image Award for Best Motion Picture Actor from the NAACP in 1969, and then started his own production company, St. Jacques Organization, Inc., in 1973.

Raymond St. Jacques' final screen appearance was in 1991's *Timebomb*, released after his cancer-related death in Los Angeles on August 27, 1990.

DAVID WATSON
(IAN CABOT, DROVER)

Not much is know about England's David Watson, so it seems fitting that his *Rawhide* character, Ian Cabot, was given no formal introduction. Sporting a striped tie instead of a bandana, he simply appears alongside Clint Eastwood in the first scene of the last season's premiere episode, "Encounter at Boot Hill." During the closing credits, he is identified as "Introducing David Watson as Ian Cabot."

Of the character, producer Ben Brady told the press, "We will take the common clichés of the West and see them through the eyes of a young Englishman. We should get lightness, a new perspective, and humor. He will add wit and charm. There were many remittance men from England who made their way out West, living on money sent them."

As it turned out, Watson was used so seldom in the season's thirteen episodes—most often not seen at all—that a viewer can only conclude that his character would have been developed in future scripts, had the series not been canceled.

After *Rawhide*, he worked almost exclusively on television, his sole Western credit a 1970 episode of *Daniel Boone*.

OTHER DROVERS

Several actors not billed as regular cast members portrayed drovers on *Rawhide* multiple times, sometimes with no screen credit:

JOHN ERWIN: Teddy in more than twenty episodes.

JOHN COLE: Bailey in more than fifteen episodes. Other TV credits: *26 Men* and *Bonanza*.

DON C. HARVEY: Collins and other characters in fourteen episodes. Other TV credits: *The Cisco Kid, The Gene Autry Show, Hopalong Cassidy, Stories of the Century, The Adventures of Kit Carson, The Roy Rogers Show, Buffalo Bill, Jr., Annie Oakley, Tales of the Texas Rangers, The Adventures of Champion, My Friend Flicka, The Adventures of Wild Bill Hickok, The Adventures of Rin Tin Tin, Death Valley Days, The Lone Ranger, 26 Men, Frontier Doctor, Colt .45, Bronco, Black Saddle, Bat Masterson, Lawman, Tombstone Territory, The Texan, Sugarfoot, Maverick, Wyatt Earp, Bonanza, Two Faces West, Wagon Train, Gunslinger, The Tall Man, Tales of Wells Fargo, Laramie, Empire, The Virginian.* Died on April 23, 1963.

JOHN HART: Narbo and other characters in seventeen episodes. Other TV credits: Replaced Clayton Moore as *The Lone Ranger* for more than fifty episodes, starred in the 1957 series *Hawkeye and the Last of the Mohicans, Tales of the Texas Rangers, Sergeant Preston of the Yukon, Cimarron City, Shotgun Slade, Bat Masterson*. Died on September 20, 2009.

HAL BAYLOR: Jenkins and other characters in over eight episodes. Other TV credits: *The Lone Ranger, Sheriff of Cochise, The Adventures of Jim Bowie, Wyatt Earp, Jefferson Drum, 26 Men, Bronco, The Californians, Maverick, The Texan, Hotel De Paree, Sugarfoot, The Alaskans, Cheyenne, Bat Masterson, The Deputy, The Rifleman, Gunslinger, Tales of Wells Fargo, Lawman, Wide Country, Have Gun-Will Travel, The Dakotas, Laramie, Wagon Train, Temple Houston, Daniel Boone, A Man Called Shenandoah, The Road West, Laredo, Pistols 'n' Petticoats, The Iron Horse, The Virginian, Death Valley Days, The Guns of Will Sonnett, Bonanza, King Fu, Gunsmoke, Barbary Coast*. Died on January 5, 1998.

WILLIAM THOMPKINS: "Toothless" Jeffries in at least nine episodes. Died in 1971.

PAUL COMI: Yo Yo in five episodes. Other TV credits: *Tombstone Territory, Two Faces West, Lawman, Wagon Train, The Tall Man, The Big Valley, The Wild Wild West, The Virginian*.

GUY TEAGUE: Stitch in at least three episodes. Also Eric Fleming's stunt double. Other TV credits: *The Adventures of Kit Carson, Zane Grey Theatre, The Adventures of Wild Bill Hickok, Maverick, Gunsmoke, Wanted Dead or Alive,*

Bat Masterson, Frontier Justice. Died January 24, 1970.

L.Q. JONES: Pee Jay in two episodes, appeared in at least three others. Other TV credits: *Cheyenne, Annie Oakley, Jefferson Drum, Black Saddle, Wichita Town, Johnny Ringo, Klondike, The Rebel, Wyatt Earp, The Americans, Two Faces West, Tales of Wells Fargo, The Rifleman, Lawman, Have Gun-Will Travel, Laramie, Empire, Wagon Train, Branded, A Man Called Shenandoah, Pistols 'n' Petticoats, Cimarron Strip, The Virginian* (semi-regular), *Hondo, The Big Valley, Lancer, Gunsmoke, Alias Smith & Jones, Kung Fu, How the West Was Won.* Given a Golden Boot Award in 2000.

CHAPTER FIVE
"MOVE 'EM OUT!"

In the early summer of 1958, Charles Marquis Warren directed "Incident at Barker Springs," the pilot episode of *Rawhide*, on California's version of the Texas plains, a generic looking Western town set, and the soundstages of TCF Television Productions. The theme music was Russ Garcia's "Beyond the Sun," heard later in every episode of the series and used over the end credits of the final season, but destined to be replaced by the famous composition by Dimitri Tiomkin and Ned Washington. Lud Gluskin, head of music for television at CBS, asked Garcia to write "some wide-open-spaces music, some chases, some fights, all sorts of music" for *Rawhide*. Garcia came up with more than a half hour of material, some of it used later in such shows as *Gunsmoke* and even the contemporary drama *Perry Mason*, but most of the background score was supplied by stock music already in the CBS archives.

The on-screen titles of the show and the episode were presented in bold capital letters rather than the rustic style that would become so recognizable, and Eric Fleming's opening narration was both longer and better than what was substituted when the pilot was altered, eliminating the formal introductions of the other cast members.

Alteration was necessitated by the decision to replace Robert Carricart, cast as the drive's superstitious Mexican cook (Cinco), with Paul Brinegar as Wishbone. (Robert Cabal would be brought in later to fill the apparent need for a superstitious Hispanic.) Scenes involving Carricart were reshot, although he was visible in at least one when the revised version was aired. The only indication that changes had been made was the shade of Fleming's hat, somewhat lighter in the new scenes.

Eastwood and Fleming in the pilot "Incident at Barker Springs."

The main flaw of the pilot was Warren's allowing the guest stars—Paul Richards, June Lockhart and DeForest Kelley—to overshadow the stars of the show, a practice that would later be instrumental in getting him fired from *The Virginian*. The cattle drive, the main subject of the series, was almost immaterial, and James Murdock—billed as Jim—was included with the guest stars in the closing credits rather than with the regular cast.

With Brinegar replacing Carricart, the network ordered additional episodes, with A.C. Lyles, a producer at Paramount Studios, listed as Associate Producer for nine episodes. Lyles was preparing to launch a series of low budget Westerns starring familiar actors past their prime, and Paramount wanted him to learn more about the genre. "I went on sort of a loan-out as a deal for CBS on a series they had some time ago," Lyles recalled more than forty years later, "and it became a big, big hit."

The *Rawhide* company headed to Nogales, Arizona, for location shooting, then returned to California for further production, headquartered at Universal-International Studios, Eastwood's former stomping ground. CBS commissioned Dimitri Tiomkin to compose show's theme song, with lyrics by Ned Washington, the vocal by Frankie Laine. All three men were familiar with Western stylings, Tiomkin having been responsible for scoring *Duel in the Sun, Red River* and *High Noon*. He and Washington had collaborated on the latter, whose theme was performed in the film by country singer Tex Ritter. Laine, however, sang the 1952 hit single, as well as the Tiomkin/Washington theme for 1957's *Gunfight at the O.K. Corral*. CBS wanted Laine's recording of the *Rawhide* theme released at least two months in advance of the show's fall debut. Ultimately, the public heard the song more than six months before finally meeting the Gil Favor outfit.

There were more than twenty Westerns on the prime time schedule in the fall of 1958, but *Rawhide* was not among them, making CBS the lone network without an hour-long representative of the genre. CBS also had the fewest number of Westerns on the air, and even though five of the six were top twenty hits (*Gunsmoke* and *Have Gun-Will Travel* numbers one and three, respectively), this evidently was deemed a sufficient amount.

Just as there are conflicting accounts as to exactly how many episodes of *Rawhide* were completed after the pilot and before production was stopped, there is some confusion regarding when CBS decided to let filming resume. Most Eastwood biographers, as well as Eastwood himself, contend that it was just before Christmas 1958. However, the December 6 issue of *TV Guide* reported: "CBS goes back into production this week with five more episodes of the hour-long *Rawhide* series, which still has failed to get a sponsor." Marlboro cigarettes—and appropriate advertising icon, the cowboy—signed on as sponsor soon after, and production moved from Universal-International to Metro-Goldwyn-Mayer Studios.

Reversing the original decision to program *Rawhide* opposite the massively popular *Wagon Train* (number two in the ratings) on Wednesday night, CBS scheduled the premiere on Friday, January 9, 1959. As is often the case (more so in 1959 than today), the pilot episode was not the first one audiences saw. Similar to the pilot, however, "Incident of the Tumbleweed" (not "Tumbleweed Wagon," as many sources state), did little to introduce or develop the regular cast, nor was the cattle drive itself essential to the plot. "Incident at Alabaster Plain," broadcast the following week, would have been a better premiere, as Fleming's opening narration named and described the supporting cast—as in the original pilot—and the actors were able to display some of the camaraderie that was to become so popular with viewers. The debut episode ranked forty-second in the weekly ratings, and *Variety* judged the first episode "a shambles." The audience obviously did not think so: by its third week on the air, *Rawhide* had risen into the top twenty, where it would remain for four seasons. Despite being on the air for only the last half, it was the number twenty-eight show of the 1958-59 season—so ranked when there were still eight episodes yet to air—with more than twenty-five million viewers tuning in. Not bad for a series the network was not certain it even wanted.

In April, the same month the seasonal ratings were posted, *Rawhide* fans were given an opportunity to see what the show would have looked like in color when *TV Guide* printed three photos for a brief feature called "Acting Up A Stampede—How a Passel of Cattle is Turned Into a Thundering Herd on *Rawhide*." Although not pictured, Eastwood, Fleming and Wooley were reported to have "joined many tons of beef along the Mexican border near Nogales, Ariz., to film a stampede."

Like the initial season of most series, the first twenty-three episodes of Rawhide varied in quality as the cast defined and developed their characters, and the writers and directors explored different avenues and textures. There was no shortage of top shelf guest stars (Martin Balsam, Dan Duryea, Jan Shepard, Lon Chaney, Jr., Brian Donlevy and Nina Foch, to name only a half dozen) or outstanding episodes, "Incident West of Lano," "Incident of the Golden Calf," and "Incident of the Dog Days" in particular.

Shortly before the next season, the September 5 issue of *TV Guide* ran another photo feature, this one entitled "Friendly Game of Pool," showing how "TV cowboys practice a watered-down version of broncobusting" on a saddle suspended from ropes over songwriter Sammy Cahn's swimming pool. The actors were Eric

Fleming (the only participant pictured alone), Clint Eastwood, Steve McQueen, Don Durant and Jock Mahoney.

Season Two began a mere nine weeks after the first concluded, with "Incident of the Day of the Dead," an offbeat choice for an opening episode, considering it featured only Rowdy Yates and had nothing to do with driving cattle. Also uncharacteristic was Eastwood doing the introductory narration rather than Eric Fleming. It is quite possible, in retrospect, that CBS was eager to capitalize on the growing popularity of Eastwood, who had been profiled by *TV Guide* the month before.

The rest of the season was not only stronger, but an improvement on the first year overall. Viewer interest in Westerns slipped somewhat, with eleven series in the top thirty as opposed to fourteen the previous season. But *Rawhide* edged up to number eighteen in the final tally, ahead of *Maverick, The Life and Legend of Wyatt Earp* and *Zane Grey Theatre*. Some of the more noteworthy episodes included "Incident of the Shambling Man" (with Victor McLaglen), "Incident of the Tinker's Dam" (with Wishbone's brother), "Incident at Sulphur Creek" (with John Dehner and Jan Shepard), and "Incident of the Deserter" (Wishbone quits). Pyro Plastics introduced a *Rawhide* Cowpuncher Model Kit, and young cowpokes could also beg their parents to buy them a plastic *Rawhide* canteen, or the first *Rawhide* comic book from Dell.

The overall popularity of Westerns continued to decline during the 1960-61 season, yet *Rawhide* finished its third year as the number six show on television, the highest position it would ever achieve. It was also Charles Marquis Warren's last season with the series, although he told the press that he had plans for the next one, specifically allowing the two top stars to alternately carry episodes. "That'll keep 'em both happy," Warren said. Similar to how he had butted heads with members of the *Gunsmoke* cast, there was friction between him and Eric Fleming, and Warren's attempts to drive a wedge between Fleming and Eastwood were not successful. In one instance, the two stars stood together when insisting that their names appear at the front of the show rather than being billed at the end. Warren claimed to be bored, as he had upon departing *Gunsmoke*, and began preparing the *Gunslinger* series several months before *Rawhide*'s third season concluded.

The show's high rating was justified by the number of exceptional episodes produced, including stories contributed by Steve Raines ("Incident at Rojo Canyon") and Sheb Wooley ("Incident of the Blackstorms"). The latter was significant in that it featured primarily the characters of Pete Nolan and Mushy, with no sign of either Gil Favor or Rowdy Yates. "Incident at Dragoon Crossing" earned the series a Western Heritage Award for fictional television drama from the National Cowboy and Western Heritage Museum, and African-American athlete/actor Woody Strode gave strong performances in two episodes, "Incident of the Buffalo Soldier" and "Incident of the Boomerang." Viewers met Mushy's mother (played by Mercedes McCambridge) in "Incident of the Captive," and "Incident of the Fish Out of Water" introduced Favor's two young daughters as well as his sister-in-law. Sheb Wooley was given more to do than in the previous two seasons, and Robert Cabal's Hey-Soos was finally billed with the rest of the regular cast.

On the marketing front, a *Rawhide* board game was released by Lowell, three more comic books were published by Dell, and in England there were three hardbound comics, called Annuals. The show was represented on the cover of *TV Guide* for the first and only time on February 4, 1961, Fleming and Eastwood both grinning for the camera. The story ("This Cowboy Feels He's Got It Made") concentrated on Eastwood, who was interviewed on MGM's Stage 22, with Fleming referred to as "deep-voiced" and "ebullient" and an actor prone to studying "the various bits and scraps of paper to which he habitually reduces his script." The article ended with Eastwood saying, "I don't figure *Rawhide* will last forever, but I don't figure to walk out on it, either."

Endre Bohem, Warren's longtime production partner, took control of *Rawhide* for the fourth season, having served as story editor, story consultant and associate producer during the previous three. Bohem put his own stamp on the series by eliminating the word "incident" from the episode titles and doing away with Eric Fleming's frequent narration altogether. Episode titles were now shown after the opening credits, with writers listed before directors. Warren had always put the director's name first.

Under Bohem's guidance, the stories began to feature the regular cast more than the guest stars, with a larger emphasis on character development rather than plot. Rowdy encountered his wayward father in "Rio Salado," the first episode of the season, Jim Quince had an uneasy reunion with his brother in "Judgment at Hondo Seco," new scout Clay Forrester was introduced in "The Inside Man," Favor's daughters and sister-in-law visited the drive in "The Boss's Daughters," in "The Deserter's Patrol" Pete Nolan ran into an Indian he freed from captivity in the third season, and Mushy met up with his cousins in "The Child-Woman." The drive was shown reaching its destination in "Abilene," which was appropriate for a season where several episodes seemed to lead into the next as opposed to occurring days apart. At the beginning of "The Sendoff," the drovers are looking for scrub cattle, a task mentioned in the previous episode.

Rawhide dropped to number thirteen in the 1961-62 ratings, yet was one of only six Westerns in the top thirty. These were busy times for the show. The script for "The Sendoff" earned the series its second Western Heritage Award; a line of *Rawhide* Western wear was introduced; Hartland Plastics released its Gil Favor and horse figurine; another hardcover annual was published in England; Dell issued a fifth comic book, and the September 2, 1961 edition of *TV Guide* ran a color photo of Fleming, Eastwood and Brinegar taking a coffee break on the set of the episode "The Woman Trap," joined by Endre Bohem, director George Templeton and guest stars Carole Kent and Karen Steele.

In February 1962, Fleming, Eastwood and Brinegar flew to Japan—where *Rawhide* was the number one show—for a four-city publicity tour sponsored by Suntory Products. Fans numbered in the thousands, forcing police to cancel parades intended to honor the American stars. Quite a bit calmer was the appearance the trio made on the CBS game show *Stump the Stars.*

Shortly before production began on the fifth season, CBS leased the seventy-acre Republic Studios for ten years, with an option to buy. For the first two years the property was shared with Four Star Films, responsible for such Western shows as *Zane Grey Theatre, Trackdown, The Rifleman, Johnny Ringo* and *The Westerner.* Rechristened CBS Studio City, the lot had some of the best exterior Western sets in town. (The buildings were used almost constantly from the 1930s through 1988, when they were torn down.) The network announced that the first series to move onto the lot would be *Rawhide*. Counting the set used for the original pilot, this was technically the fourth time the production had moved in four years.

Endre Bohem left the series after only one season, replaced by producer Vincent M. Fennelly, no stranger to Westerns. Among his credits were *Trackdown, Wanted Dead or Alive* and numerous films throughout the 1950s. While the opening title scenes of *Rawhide* had always varied somewhat from week to week, Fennelly replaced them with a map of the different cattle trails, a series of dashes indicating where the Gil Favor outfit was headed. For season five, the destination was Denver, along the Goodnight/Loving Trail. Resumed in 1962 was the word "incident" in the episode titles, shown in the middle of the screen instead of the lower right, where it had been located during the first three years. Fennelly continued Bohem's practice of developing the supporting cast and giving them more to do, obvious right from the first episode, "Incident of the Hunter," in which Quince revealed that he may be a wanted man in Oklahoma. Even in "Incident of the Portrait" (one of the best episodes of the entire series), which focuses mainly on guest stars John Ireland and Nina Shipman, there was an effort to involve all the regulars, though Charles Gray did not appear. Other memorable stories of the season included "Incident of the Dogfaces" (with James Whitmore), "Incident of the Trail's End" (with Harold J. Stone), "Incident of Judgment Day" (with Claude Rains) and "Incident of the White Eyes" (with Nehemiah Persoff).

The 1962-63 season was not a particularly good one for Westerns, with *Bonanza* and *Gunsmoke* the only two in the top ten. *Rawhide* fell to twenty-second, slightly ahead of such fading classics as *Wagon Train* and *Have Gun-Will Travel.* The newest entry, NBC's ninety-minute *The Virginian*, with Charles Marquis Warren as executive producer or simply producer of eleven episodes, came in at number twenty-six.

Most television historians regard the following season as the sunset of the Western genre, although *Bonanza*, with an audience share of nearly thirty-seven million, was number two in the ratings. *The Virginian* crept up to seventeen, but the sturdy *Gunsmoke*, in its third year as an hour-long show, fell to number twenty. *Rawhide's*

Eastwood and Fleming.

position was even more alarming: forty-fourth, unwisely moved to Thursday night and up against the popular sitcoms *The Donna Reed Show* and *My Three Sons* on ABC. Still produced by Fennelly, its sixth season proved to be the last consistent one. Yet another opening sequence was employed, with the drive shown crossing a desert, and silhouettes of Fleming, Eastwood and Brinegar under their names. Although promoted to scout at the end of the previous season, Steve Raines continued to be listed with the rest of the supporting cast. Despite its dwindling audience, there were a number of strong episodes, among them "Incident of the Red Wind," "Incident of the Travellin' Man," "Incident at Farragut Pass," "Incident at Ten Trees" and "Incident of Iron Bull," which earned the series its third Western Heritage Award. The network wisely showed a light-hearted episode, "Incident at Confidence Creek," the week following President John F. Kennedy's assassination. The fifth season also included the show's first two-part episode, "Incident at Dead Horse." Nor was there a shortage of talented guests: Neville Brand, James Whitmore, Simon Oakland, Elizabeth Montgomery, Burgess Meredith, Mickey Rooney and Broderick Crawford. Unfortunately, the season concluded with "Incident of the Peyote Cup," one of the series' weaker offerings.

Despite a Golden Globe nomination, the 1963-64 season may well have been the show's swansong if not for the intervention of CBS chairman William S. Paley, a fan of Westerns, *Rawhide* in particular. (Paley was allegedly instrumental in convincing a reluctant Richard Boone to do a sixth year of *Have Gun-Will Travel*, but could not get the actor to go along with expanding the series to an hour. In 1967, Paley overruled the network programmer's cancelation of *Gunsmoke*, which went on to run for eight more seasons.)

After singing with Buddy Ebsen and Fess Parker on *The Danny Kaye Show*, Clint Eastwood flew to Rome to make *A Fistful of Dollars* while *Rawhide* was on hiatus, returning to find that Vincent Fennelly and story consultant Paul King had left to develop NBC's upcoming *Daniel Boone*. In their place were producers Bruce Geller and Bernard Kowalski, with Robert E. Thompson as associate producer. All three had some experience writing for Westerns, but their decision to reinvent *Rawhide* as a mostly dark character study rather than the story of a cattle drive was wrongheaded. "They were competent," Fleming said later. "They worked their butts off, but they produced bombs." And as often happened during Warren's tenure, the guest stars elbowed the regular cast, as well as the beeves, off to the side in too many episodes. The show was moved back to Friday, scheduled against the animated *Jonny Quest* and the sitcom *The Farmer's Daughter* on ABC, and *International Showtime* on NBC, none of which were big hits. Even so, *Rawhide* remained stuck at number forty-four in the ratings.

The public's taste for Westerns had long since been satisfied by oversaturation and familiarity. Blessed by a colorful and versatile cast, imaginative writers, and managing to become more than just a Western, *Bonanza*, now the number one show on television, was an exception. Elsewhere, the novelty of *The Virginian*'s ninety-minute format had worn off to a degree, the show sliding down to number twenty-two, and *Gunsmoke* ranked twenty-seventh, an all-time low for what was still the most authentic Western on the air. (A midseason surprise was *Branded*, which returned *The Rifleman*'s Chuck Connors to the video prairie. It was the fourteenth most popular show of the 1964-65 season, but in its second [and final] year, did not make the top thirty at all.)

During the seventh season, many of the qualities that had made *Rawhide* such a success were lacking. The cast seldom interacted, and both Rocky Shahan and Robert Cabal had been fired. Fleming and Eastwood were often singled out for their own stories, but with guest stars usually taking center stage. In "Canliss," which featured a rare dramatic appearance by Dean Martin, the drovers are barely necessary. "Damon's Road," a semi-comedic story stretched to two weeks, was atypically tedious, and too many episodes took place in towns, a setting viewers had objected to since the very beginning of the series. There were exceptions, such as "Corporal Dasovik," which netted *Rawhide* its fourth Western Heritage Award, "The Race," "The Lost Herd," "The Photographer," "A Man Called Mushy," "Mrs. Harmon," and "No Dogs or Drovers." The latter earned an Eddie Award from the American Cinema Editors.

Geller and Kowalski turned out twenty-one episodes—not all broadcast consecutively—before CBS decided the show's new direction was not working. The network gave the producers their walking papers, and then brought Endre Bohem back to see if the rest of the season could be salvaged. The first thing Bohem did was rehire Sheb Wooley, Rocky Shahan and Robert Cabal for the remaining nine episodes, most of which recaptured the old *Rawhide* flavor. "Texas Fever," "Prairie Fire," "The Empty Sleeve" and "The Calf Women" were especially good. However, the season ended on a sour note with "The Gray Rock Hotel," a leftover from the Geller/ Kowalski regime, and possibly the most bizarre segment in the history of the series. Suffering from a mysterious illness, the drovers take refuge in an abandoned hotel whose sole resident is a woman who hates men, has killed her husband, and is hiding from her husband's friends. In the words of noted Kentucky playwright and historian Lanny Tucker: "When I first saw the episode I thought to myself, '*This* is *Rawhide?*'"

As early as February, James T. Aubrey, president of CBS-TV since late 1959, decided once again to cancel *Rawhide*. However, he was replaced the following month, and the series was back on the schedule. Ben Brady, fresh from overseeing the second (and abbreviated) season of ABC's *The Outer Limits*, became the latest in the revolving door of *Rawhide* producers. Although he was best known for his long association with *Perry Mason*, he had also been involved with *Have Gun-Will Travel* and presumably knew something about how to produce a Western. Instead of attempting to change the tone of *Rawhide*, as his predecessors had done, Brady made the ultimately unwise decision to revamp the cast. Of the eight original regulars, only Eastwood, Brinegar and Raines remained. Asked why Raines stayed but Sheb Wooley had not, Brady responded, "They duplicated each other. We dropped Wooley because he was more expensive than Raines." Also gone for good were Rocky Shahan, James Murdock and Robert Cabal. The most drastic change was the departure of Eric Fleming, his absence a palpable loss in the final season. There was no mention of what happened to Gil Favor, leaving viewers to conclude that he had finally bought his own cattle ranch and settled down with his daughters, the task of training Rowdy to take over evidently complete. Eastwood reluctantly agreed to headline the show by himself.

In June, *TV Guide* announced that "British actor-singer David Watson joins the cast of regulars in next season's revised *Rawhide*." Also added were Raymond St. Jacques as drover Solomon King, and John Ireland as scout Jed Colby. The three actors were rarely used in the same episode.

When a network executive told the press that in spite of the changes to the cast, everything was still the same, Brady was irate. "It is *not* the same show," he insisted. "We've got to get people to realize it's not." Although he retained the title of executive producer, Brady decided he was not interested in the day-to-day production of *Rawhide*, leaving the network in a last minute scramble to find a show runner. The first candidate approached was Endre Bohem, and he accepted initially. Eager to inject some new creative blood into the series, he proposed moving the setting to 19th century Hawaii, then backed off running the show entirely. The task of guiding the show through its last days fell to Robert E. Thompson, who had been marginally involved with the production of the seventh season. In addition to doing some acting and writing for both films and television (*Wagon Train, Bonanza, Have Gun-Will Travel*), he had produced the 1963-64 Western series *The Travels of Jamie McPheeters* and penned "Josh," one of the better episodes of *Rawhide's* erratic seventh season.

If regular viewers considered the majority of the previous season to be markedly different from the show they had followed loyally since January 1959, the final thirteen episodes required a greater degree of acceptance that, in the end, was not forthcoming. There was a return to the spirit of camaraderie among the drovers that had been largely missing, but absent now were too many familiar faces. "The nucleus of the old audience will be disappointed," Paul Brinegar told a reporter. And though the storylines were for the most part back on track, concentrating more on the drive rather than what occurred away from it, some of the writing was less than top drawer. Steve Raines, now the ramrod, went so far as to tell the press that the scripts he was getting were "mediocre."

While producing *The Outer Limits,* Ben Brady was quoted as saying, "On every series you look at, the production operation knows that out of sixteen episodes, say, four might be good ones. Five, if you're lucky. And most of the rest is run of the mill."

As for the last thirteen episodes of *Rawhide,* the majority were indeed "run of the mill," at least four of them below average. Nevertheless, they were loaded with such outstanding guests as Albert Dekker, Charles Bronson, Ralph Bellamy and Mercedes McCambridge, as well as Western favorites Warren Oates, Bruce Dern, Claude Akins, Rory Calhoun, Jim Davis, Johnny Crawford and Dick Foran. Unfortunately, the actors were often better than the stories in which they appeared.

"Encounter at Boot Hill," the first episode of the season, began with a teaser rather than the opening credits for the first time in the show's history. The credits themselves were accompanied by new pen and ink drawings of various Western characters and a re-recorded rendition of the famous theme, still sung by Frankie Laine. The rustic *Rawhide* logo, however, was gone. Steve Raines was finally given star billing along with Eastwood and Brinegar, as well as Raymond St. Jacques. Following the first commercial break, Ben Brady was top billed as executive producer, with Robert E. Thompson listed merely as producer. The episode, directed by television veteran Sutton Roley, featured close-ups and odd camera angles. The industry doubtlessly took notice as editor Gene Fowler, Jr. earned an Eddie nomination for Best Edited Television Program at the end of the season. While interesting to look at, "Encounter at Boot Hill" was long on exposition and short on action, hardly an auspicious season opener for a series struggling for survival. What action took place occurred with nary a cow in sight. Nor did the episode conclude with the signature cry of "head 'em up, move 'em out!" At one point, Rowdy, now surlier as trail boss than as ramrod, remarks, "Everything changes eventually. It changes or it dies." *Rawhide* had definitely changed. And it was dying.

In truth, the television Western in general was ailing by the time of the 1965-66 season. *Gunsmoke* fell out of the top twenty in the annual ratings for the second year in a row, coming in at number thirty. Not much better were *The Virginian* (in a three-way finish at number twenty-three with *The Jackie Gleason Show* and the gimmicky newcomer *The Wild Wild West*) and *Daniel Boone*, three notches lower. Only the apparently invincible *Bonanza*, in its seventh season, was an unquestionable success, rated the most popular show in the country for the second year in a row. A *Bonanza*-like family Western, *The Big Valley*, debuted and would run for four seasons, due mainly to the presence of Barbara Stanwyck and *Black Saddle's* rugged Peter Breck. The second season of Chuck Connors' *Branded* failed to attract even half of its original audience despite switching to color. Three new series—*The Legend of Jesse James, A Man Called Shenandoah, The Loner*—were respectable efforts but lasted only one season. NBC's sole new Western, *Laredo*, a spin-off from *The Virginian*, was more successful, returning for a second season in 1966.

Rawhide may have also fared better had CBS not vetoed a proposal to shoot the eighth season in color, or moved the show to Tuesday night, opposite the ABC hit *Combat!*, which had ranked in

Eastwood and Fleming.

the top ten the year before. Even before completing the final few
episodes, the cast realized the end was near.

The eighth season did have its moments, including "Ride a Crooked
Mile" (introducing John Ireland as scout Jed Colby and a typically
quirky performance by John Drew Barrymore), "Six Weeks to Bent
Fork" (Wishbone admires the new trail boss and observes, "It looks
like Rowdy Yates is growin' whiskers") and "Escort to Doom"

(Wishbone reveals he had a younger brother killed by Indians). In the otherwise ordinary "Clash at Broken Bluff," Rowdy mentions that he had a stepmother he did not like and was relieved when she died. In "Crossing at White Feather" he says he does not know where his father is, or if he is alive—a contradiction to the events of 1961's "Rio Salado," in which Rowdy's father is killed. Evidently no one, including Eastwood, was concerned about continuity by this time.

Coincidentally, "Crossing at White Feather," the last episode of the series, was directed by Richard Whorf, who in 1958 had directed "Incident of the Tumbleweed," the first one to air. Appropriately, one of the final sequences depicted the drovers moving the herd along, with Rowdy urging, "All right, Blake, move 'em out! Keep 'em rollin'! Keep movin' 'em across!" The closing shot of the series was a close-up of Eastwood, whose agent had managed to get CBS to pay his client for a full season of thirty episodes, seventeen of which were never filmed.

Regarding the cancelation of *Rawhide*, producer Robert E. Thompson later remarked, "No one, I would venture not even Paley by then, shed many tears at its demise. The show had more than run its course by then."

Television's longest-running cattle drive had begun halfway through a season, January 1959, and ended at the same point, with a rerun on January 4, 1966.

PART TWO

EPISODE GUIDE

SEASON ONE

There were 217 episodes of *Rawhide* produced from mid-1958 to late 1965. After being shown in syndication for several years, CBS released fifty episodes available by mail subscription through Columbia House, its home entertainment division, beginning in 1990. Six episodes were released to the general market on individual VHS tapes. In recent years, the FX and Hallmark cable channels have run the series in its entirety, although edited, sometimes severely. However, each channel often cut different scenes, making it possible to view episodes nearly intact if fans recorded both versions. To date, the first three seasons have been released on DVD by CBS/Paramount.

Rawhide employed more than forty directors, most frequently Thomas Carr, Ted Post, Jesse Hibbs and Christian Nyby. Scripts and/or stories were contributed by over eighty different writers, the majority from John Dunkel, Louis Vittes, and Charles Larson. Actors Eric Fleming, Sheb Wooley, Steve Raines and Michael Pate also had a hand in the writing.

The show's main producers were Charles Marquis Warren, Endre Bohem, Vincent M. Fennelly, Bruce Geller, Bernard Kowlski, Ben Brady and Robert E. Thompson, with assistance from Paul King, Ernest Nims, Del Reisman and A.C. Lyles.

Most of the music was contributed by eight different composers, chiefly Dimitri Tiomkin, Russ Garcia, Leon Klatzkin, Fred Steiner and Hugo Friedhofer. Herschel Burke Gilbert, executive music director for CBS, won a Western Heritage Award for the score of the 1964 episode "Damon's Road."

The spectacular and dangerous stunts were performed by no less than twenty athletic and courageous souls, including such legends as Whitey Hughes, Bob Hoy and Hal Needham. Cast members Rocky Shahan, Steve Raines, John Cole, Guy Teague and Bill Thompkins also got in on the action.

And for history's sake, Gil Favor's horse was named Butch. Rowdy Yates rode Midnight.

* * * * * *

The episode guide for *Rawhide* is presented chronologically, in order by first-run air date (*not* order of production).

#1: INCIDENT OF THE TUMBLEWEED
(JANUARY 9, 1959)

DIRECTOR: Richard Whorf
STORY: Curtis Kenyon
TELEPLAY: Fred Freiberger
CAST: Terry Moore, John Larch, Tom Conway, Val
             Dufour, Frank Wilcox, Maurice Manson, David
             Whorf, Bob Steele, Bill Hale, John War Eagle

NARRATION: "It's not the roundin' up and the ropin' and the brandin' of the cattle that's the big problems of the ranchers. It's getting' 'em to market. Fifteen hundred bone-weary miles from the southern tip of Texas to the railhead at Sedalia. That's where I come in. Gil Favor's my name. Trail boss."

Gil Favor and Rowdy Yates encounter seven criminals, including a woman, being transported to prison in an enclosed wagon, as well as the outlaws attempting to free them.

NOTES: Generic cattle opening, with no recognizable actors. Mushy is introduced as possibly feeble minded, Wishbone cantankerous. More concentration on the guests than the regulars, who make token appearances and have little to say or do.

Fleming and Terry Moore in "Incident of the Tumbleweed."

#2: INCIDENT AT ALABASTER PLAIN
(JANUARY 16, 1959)

DIRECTOR: Richard Whorf

WRITER: David Swift

CAST: Mark Richman, Martin Balsam, Troy Donahue, Joe De Santis, Suzanne Lloyd, Peter Marmakos

NARRATION: "A thousand miles from San Antone to the railhead at Sedalia, Missouri. We got three thousand head of Texas cattle that don't want to go. When everything's right we cover eight miles a day. But how often are things right? The weather's what hits you the hardest between the eyes. Boiling sun that dries up the water, brings the dust and sand. Storms that mill the cattle, touch off stampedes. The way the land lies can hurt you, too, wearing off pounds with every step the beeves take. But the way to even things up is to hire the best men in the business. I got 'em. Pete Nolan, scout. Rowdy Yates, new as they come, but he's got the makings. Joe Scarlett, swing. Jim Quince, flank. And the man who can make or break the drive—the cook, Wishbone. And the cook's louse—his name is Mushy. And somebody's gotta kick this whole kit and caboodle along. That's me. Gil Favor, trail boss. I ride point."

The drovers are invited to the wedding of Rowdy's friend Buzz, but the festivities are disrupted by a band of outlaws led by the bride's brother.

NOTES: A slightly different opening, Eastwood and Shahan recognizable. Favor says the traditional ending, "Head 'em up, move 'em out" for the first time, but they are not his final words; he has a conversation with Pete and Rowdy afterwards. No sign of Mushy except during opening narration, although listed in closing credits. Would have been a better premiere episode.

#3: INCIDENT WITH AN EXECUTIONER
(JANUARY 23, 1959)

DIRECTOR: Charles Marquis Warren
WRITER: James Edmiston
CAST: Dan Duryea, Martin Milner, Marguerite Chapman, James Drury, Jan Shepard, Stafford Repp, William Schallert, Glen Gordon

NARRATION: "On the Sedalia Trail, pushing a herd of three thousand mixed head, you're always a long ways from nowhere. Ahead—trouble, known and unknown. Behind—owners depending on the drive, counting on men crazy enough to push it. Like me—Gil Favor, trail boss."

Gil and Rowdy come across a group of stranded stagecoach passengers who are being threatened by a mysterious gunslinger who has targeted one of them, but won't say who.

NOTES: Third opening, with individual shots of the actors that were used along with Fleming's narration in the previous episode. Wishbone shown smoking his beloved pipe for the first time. Also the first episode to end with "Head 'em up, move 'em out!" A somewhat confusing story that attempts to achieve more than the running time allows.

#4: INCIDENT OF THE WIDOWED DOVE
(JANUARY 30, 1959)

DIRECTOR: Ted Post
WRITER: David Lang
CAST: Jay C. Flippen, Sally Forrest, Harry Shannon, Vic Perrin, Harry Lauter, Fred Graham, Harry Harvey Sr., Dick Ryan, Henry Wills

NARRATION: "The Sedalia Trail is a thousand miles of dust, deep river crossings and stampedes, a job forgotten by those who wait for their cattle at the end of the drive. But not forgotten by the men in the saddle who bring the cattle through. Like me—Gil Favor, trail boss."

The drive takes a break in the town of Tascoa Junction, Favor warning his men that the drinks are watered and the games crooked. Rowdy becomes involved with a saloon girl desperate to get away from her husband—the town's marshal.

NOTES: Back to the same opening as the premiere. First episode to feature Rowdy. First of Harry Lauter's twelve episodes. A fly can be seen on Favor's hat in the jail scene. Title gives away the ending.

#5: INCIDENT ON THE EDGE OF MADNESS
(FEBRUARY 6, 1959)

DIRECTOR: Andrew V. McLaglen
WRITERS: Herbert Little Jr. & David Victor
CAST: Lon Chaney Jr., Marie Windsor, Alan Marshall, Ralph Reed, Duane Grey, Fay Roope, Jester Hairston, George Hickman

NARRATION: "Cattle drive's mostly hard work, doin' without, bein' alone. It's warmin' yourself in a rainstorm with no fuel but buffalo chips, spreadin' your duds on an anthill to get rid of the vermin. It's bein' and doin' things you don't rightly aks of two-legged humans, unless they're cowboys. Add discipline and loyalty to the list, all for thirty dollars a month. It's a big strain on a man. You have to expect something to give along the way, and bust wide open. I'm in a position to know. I'm Gil Favor, trail boss."

Favor and Rowdy find themselves abandoned by the rest of the men when a Southern gentleman and a former saloon girl from New Orleans persuade them to help establish a new Confederacy in South America.

NOTES: First episode to deal with the drive. Duane Grey was one of the candidates for the role of Pete Nolan. The drowning of the "Boston" character based on an actual 1866 incident. First of Lon Chaney's two appearances and Marie Windsor's three.

#6: INCIDENT OF THE POWER AND THE PLOW
(FEBRUARY 13, 1959)

DIRECTOR: Victor V. McLaglen
WRITER: Fred Freiberger
CAST: Brian Donlevy, Rudolfo Acosta, Dick Van Patten,
              Malcom Atterbury, Michael Pate, Jeanne Bates,
              Carol Thurston, Sandy Kenyon, Robert Gist

NARRATION: "The Sedalia Trail's as rough as it is long. You might say deuces are wild the way everything comes in twos. In the low country, two inches of rain in half an hour. Coming through the passes it was two feet of snow. On this side of the mountains we had two brushes with rustlers. Ended up burying two hands. Now it's been two days since grass and water. But my job's to kick this herd along no matter what. The only way I know to get a thing done is to keep trying. Gil Favor's my name, trail boss."

The drive comes upon a sign reading: "Jed Reston's Land—Stay Out If You Ain't Been Asked In." Reston, a wealthy and bigoted rancher, offers five dollars to any man who will whip a Comanche accused of stealing a cow.

NOTES: Michael Pate, who would later write an episode, made five appearances on *Rawhide*. He was a regular contributor to *Western Clippings* until his death in his native Australia on September 1, 2008. He was 88.

#7 (PILOT EPISODE): INCIDENT AT BARKER SPRINGS (FEBRUARY 20, 1959)

DIRECTOR: Charles Marquis Warren
WRITER: Les Crutchfield
CAST: Richard Gilden, DeForest Kelley, Bill Hale, Paul Richards, June Lockhart

ORIGINAL PILOT NARRATION: "On a drive from San Antone to Sedalia, I don't have to remind myself what's lyin' in wait for us up ahead. But sometimes I'm apt to forget what we've left behind. This isn't a single brand herd—it's made up of a lot of brands, a hundred small owners counting on us to get through. A hundred small ranches that'll be dust next year if we don't make it. A late season start—the early herds have first call on the weather. But not the top riders, and they make the difference. I hand picked every one of my boys, and they can ride with the best. Pete Nolan, swing. Joe Scarlett, flank. Jim Quince, point. Rowdy Yates, brand new but eager. And most important, Cinco, a cook who can cook. And a cook's louse—his name is Mushy. One thing sure—a trail boss who thinks he can push a drive through this late has to be out of his mind. But somebody's got to be fool enough to try it. And that's me—Gil Favor, trail boss."

REVISED NARRATION: "On a drive from San Antone to Sedalia I don't have to remind myself what's lying in wait for us up ahead. But sometimes I'm apt to forget what we've left behind. This isn't a single brand herd—it's made up of a lot of brands, a hundred small owners counting on us to get through. The early herds have first call on the weather. We get the grazed out, parched lands, dry enough for a bolt of lightning to touch off a prairie fire. Streams too thin to plow, but too thick to drink. One thing's sure—a trail boss who thinks he can drive through this late has to be out of his mind. But somebody's got to try it. And that's me—Gil Favor, trail boss."

June Lockhart and Fleming in "Incident at Barker Springs."

When a young drover is killed by a ruthless rancher, Favor and Rowdy join the drover's brother, a hired gun, in seeking vengeance.

NOTES: The first of Paul Richards' two appearances on the show. Fine, understated acting by June Lockhart. Robert Carricart, whom Paul Brinegar replaced as the drive's cook, can be spotted briefly.

#8: INCIDENT WEST OF LANO
(FEBRUARY 27, 1959)

DIRECTOR: Charles Marquis Warren
WRITER: Buckley Angell
CAST: Martha Hyer, Robert H. Harris, Nancy Hadley,
              James Anderson, Abby Dalton, Jacqueline Mayo,
              Ron Soble, K.L. Smith

NARRATION: "I got a cousin, woman, teaches in a school house back East. She tells me those boys daydream about becomin' cowboys. Of all the jobs a man could pick, why'd he ever want to choose this way to make a livin'? Three thousand head of God's lowest form of life, cattle. If they don't die of tick fever, strangle in a dust storm or trample their fool selves to death, then the market'll go down to two cents a pound on the hoof. They might as well have died before we set out. But they need food back East. It's my job to get this herd movin'. My name's Gil Favor, trail boss."

Pete finds a steer butchered by four women living in a broken down show wagon: The Haley Sisters—Sharpshooters, Knife Throwers and Fancy Roping Artists. Favor warns them about Comanches, but their real trouble is a mean bunch of freighters determined to get their wagons across the river ahead of Favor's herd.

NOTES: One of the best episodes of the first season, but not the first one filmed, as has been reported by some sources. First of four episodes with Ron Soble, who was given a Golden Boot Award shortly before his death at 74 in 2002.

#9: INCIDENT OF THE TOWN IN TERROR
(MARCH 6, 1959)

DIRECTOR: Ted Post
WRITER: Oliver Crawford
CAST: Margaret O'Brien, Harry Townes, Don C. Harvey,
              Pat O'Moore, Russ Conway, Kem Dibbs, Dan
              White, James Gavin, Gary Walberg

NARRATION: "Ridin' herd over a long trail may be a headache, but I can tell you it's never boresome, even when it's goin' smooth. There's plenty of sweet grass, blue skies, clear spring water. You ride lazy, thinkin' of what you left behind, dreamin' of what's ahead. Ridin' easy doesn't come often on a drive. When you're pushin' three thousand head and twenty hands, there's always something about to happen. Whatever it is, and whenever it comes up, I gotta meet it. That's my job. I'm Gil Favor, trail boss."

Rowdy comes down with the same fever plaguing a number of the cattle, but the citizens of a nearby town will not allow the drovers or the herd to enter. The daughter of the pharmacist is the sole person willing to come to Rowdy's aid.

NOTES: Favor does not say "Head 'em up, move 'em out!" Margaret O'Brien was a successful child actress most remembered for 1944's *Meet Me in St. Louis*. She also appeared in an episode of *Wagon Train*.

#10: INCIDENT OF THE GOLDEN CALF
(MARCH 13, 1959)

DIRECTOR: Jesse Hibbs
WRITER: Endre Bohem
CAST: Macdonald Carey, Charles Gray, John Pickard, Richard Shannon, Chuck Roberson, Clem Fuller

NARRATION: "Breeding ground of the cattle is the southern tip of Texas, and the markets are over a thousand miles away. A day's drive on the Sedalia Trail is eight, ten miles at the most. Fine and easy when the prairie grass is fresh and the river's wet. But you have to keep goin' when the grasses are parched, when the water has disappeared under the drought. That's when the cows become skittish, hard to manage. Nobody takes his boots off as long as it lasts. The last one to take his boots off is me—Gil Favor, trail boss."

Just as another trail boss is plotting to take over the herd, most of Favor's men decide to go looking for gold.

NOTES: Very good episode written by story editor and future producer Bohem. First of two appearances by Charles Gray before joining the cast. Favor says it is his first time on the Sedalia Trail. Wishbone says the three things he is proudest of are his sourdough cake, his beard and his poker playing.

#11: Incident of the Coyote Weed
(March 20, 1959)

Director: Jesse Hibbs
Writer: David Lang
Cast: Rick Jason, Buzz Martin, James Gavin, Kem Dibbs, Gary Wallberg, Jorge Moreno

Narration: "Pushin' cattle up the Sedalia Trail's a thousand miles of aching bones and deep madness. You lose a lot of men. Some men never make it. Sometimes you don't rightly think a man was ever born who could. Well, men fool you sometimes, especially on a cattle drive. I ought to know. My name's Gil Favor, trail boss."

Most of the outfit is poisoned by coyote weed deliberately put in their food at the same time they are being menaced by a gang of Mexican bandits.

Notes: A grave marker for a drover killed in a stampede indicates the year as being 1868. Sheb Wooley and Paul Brinegar are paired in the closing credits. Rick Jason went on to television stardom in the *Combat!* series. First episode filmed at MGM.

#12: Incident of the Chubasco
(April 3, 1959)

Director: Al C. Ward
Writer: Buzz Kulik
Cast: George Brent, John Ericson, Noah Berry, Olive Sturgess, Stacy Harris

Narration: "On a drive the days and nights get mighty big. There's a lot of danger a man can understand, and a lot he can't. That's the kind I hate, the kind I can't understand. I'm Gil Favor, trail boss."

A young woman flees from her abusive husband, a powerful rancher, and takes refuge with the drive. Her husband tells Favor he has enough dynamite to close a mountain trail the herd must pass through unless his wife is returned.

Notes: George Brent was a major star during Hollywood's golden age, appearing in such classic films as *Jezebel, Dark Victory* and *The*

Spiral Staircase. He continued working until his death in 1979. *Rawhide* was his only television Western role.

#13: INCIDENT OF THE CURIOUS STREET
(APRIL 10, 1959)

DIRECTOR: Ted Post
ORIGINAL STORY: N.B. Stone, Jr.
TELEPLAY: Earl Baldwin & N.B. Stone
CAST: Mercedes McCambridge, James Westerfield,
                   Whitney Blake, Dennis Cross, Ralph Moody

NARRATION: "When a man's pushing ornery cows over the Sedalia Trail, he's gotta hope for the best, expect the worst. You never know what the cows'll do—it keeps a man jumping, always on the watch. But I wouldn't trade the job. I'm Gil Favor, trail boss."

Gil and Rowdy ride into a ghost town where a woman and her daughter are being held captive by outlaws.

NOTES: Slightly different opening, with all the principals clearly identified. Third reference to Rowdy having been in a Union prison. First utterance of Wishbone's famous "mighty well told." Rowdy says "Head 'em up, move 'em out" for the first time when Favor tells him to take over. Mercedes McCambridge was in four episodes, once as Mushy's mother.

#14: INCIDENT OF THE DOG DAYS
(APRIL 17, 1959)

DIRECTOR: George Sherman
WRITER: Samuel A. Peeples
CAST: Don Dubbins, R.G. Armstrong, Addison Richards,
            Ross Elliott, John Vivyan, Craig Duncan, Milan
            Smith, Hal Roth

NARRATION: "Every once in a while you have to get away from the herd, so you can listen to the sound of it. You can tell a lot from the way the cattle bawl. But the same can't be said for the drovers you hire along the way. It's hard to judge a man by his voice. That's why we keep gainin' some, losin' others. It's my job to judge, and sometimes I miss. My name's Gil Favor, trail boss."

An older trail boss warns Favor that the drive is trying to cross a forty mile bad stretch at the wrong time of year. A detour might take as many as three weeks, so Favor decides to go ahead anyway.

NOTES: A classic episode, but with more phony exteriors than usual. Favor does not order the men to "head 'em up, move 'em out" at the end. The cattle simply drink and move along as a clap of thunder is heard. R.G. Armstrong guest starred on more than thirty television Westerns, including four episodes of *Rawhide*. He was honored with a well deserved Golden Boot Award in 1999.

#15: INCIDENT OF THE CALICO GUN
(APRIL 24, 1959)

DIRECTOR: Jesse Hibbs
WRITER: Winston Miller
CAST: Gloria Talbott, Jack Lord, Myron Healey, Gene
             Collins, Steve Mitchell, Damian O'Flynn

NARRATION: "You run into a lot of things on a cattle drive before you get where you're goin'. Stampedes, floods, sickness. But one thing's with you all the time. You can't get away from it, you can't lick it—the same faces day after day, week after week. You look at each other, or you look at the cattle. After a while you can't tell the difference. I'm getting that way myself. My name's Gil Favor, trail boss."

Rowdy feels he is falling in love with a young woman Pete and Favor have rescued from a burning ranch house, unaware that she is being used as bait by a band of outlaws planning to rob the drovers.

NOTES: Favor remarks that Rowdy will be a trail boss one day. Rowdy mentions his father for the first time. Gloria Talbott was also in Charles Marquis Warren's *Cattle Empire* as well as numerous television Westerns, including two episodes of *Rawhide*. She died in 2000 at the age of 69. Jack Lord also made two episodes of *Rawhide* and starred in the modern Western series *Stoney Burke*. The longtime *Hawaii Five-O* star died in 1998, aged 77.

Jack Lord and Gloria Talbott in "Incident of the Calico Gun."

#16: INCIDENT OF THE MISPLACED INDIANS
(MAY 1, 1959)

DIRECTOR: Jesse Hibbs
WRITERS: David Victor & Herbert Little, Jr.
CAST: Kim Hunter, Lyle Talbot, Virginia Gregg, Richard
             Hale, Robert Carson, Milan Smith, Rodd Redwing
NARRATION: "Pointing 'em north, most things you can calculate. Your men, for instance. You know what to expect. But there's one

thing you can't calculate on—the people who cross your trail. The thousand ways they can make their troubles yours. You find that out real quick in my job. My name's Gil Favor, trail boss."

Rowdy finds two dead Delaware Indians outside a ranch house where the woman inside is singing and making candy.

NOTES: Second episode involving poison. Good performance by Kim Hunter, best known for her work in *The Seventh Victim, A Streetcar Named Desire* and *Planet of the Apes*. She died in 2002, aged 79.

#17: INCIDENT OF FEAR IN THE STREETS
(MAY 8, 1959)

DIRECTOR: Andrew V. McLaglen
WRITER: Fred Freiberger
CAST: Gary Merrill, Robert Driscoll, Corey Allen, Morris
              Ankrum, Don Haggerty, Whit Bissell, Bob Steele,
              Eleanor Ayer, Ed Nelson, Ed Faulkner, Olan Soule,
              Guy Stockwell, Amzie Strickland, Len Hendry

NARRATION: "Ask any townsman along the Sedalia, Missouri Trail and he'll tell you that drovers are nothin' but trouble. They work hard, play hard, fight hard. They're sons of the devil. But if you want to hear their side, just ask me. Favor's my name, trail boss.

When Pete is gored by one of the beeves, Favor and Rowdy ride to the nearest town to get a doctor. They are prevented from getting back to Pete until two fugitives in hiding are found and hanged.

NOTES: Loaded with familiar character actors, but one of the town-bound episodes fans of the show objected to, wanting to see more of the cattle drive.

#18: INCIDENT BELOW THE BRAZOS
(MAY 15, 1959)

DIRECTOR: Jack Arnold
WRITER: Herbert Purdum
CAST: Leslie Nielsen, Kathleen Crowley, Martin Landau,

Irene Tedrow, Robert Cabal, William Joyce, John
Craven, Alan Reynolds

NARRATION: "In the trail towns they say the only thing wilder than
Texas steers are the cowhands who drive 'em. So if a big herd is
gonna reach the market, there has to be someone tough enough to
handle the crew and the cattle and anything else that might get in
the way during a thousand slow, grinding miles. And it's a job, and
it's mine. Gil Favor's my name, trail boss."

A group of farmers warns the drive to steer clear of their land.
When one of the homesteaders is trampled to death by the drive's
remuda, his family tries to hang Favor.

NOTES: First appearance of Robert Cabal as wrangler Hey-Soos.
Rocky Shahan is given his biggest scene to date. Jack Arnold directed
the 1955 sci-fi film *Tarantula*, in which Eastwood had a small
part.

#19: INCIDENT OF THE DRY DRIVE
(MAY 22, 1959)

DIRECTOR: Andrew V. McLaglen
WRITER: John Dunkel
CAST: Victor Jory, Jean Inness, Ron Hagerthy, Chris
              Alcaide

NARRATION: "Bringin' a heard up through the plains of Texas on the
Sedalia, Missouri Trail, you need three things: One of them, air, we
have more than enough of. Another, grass, usually in good supply.
But the third is another story. It's always with us, the need for water.
Sometimes it's a real job to find it. And it's my job. Gil Favor, trail
boss."

Favor accuses a former trail boss Jess Hode of stealing some of his
beeves. Hode claims the cattle were strays, then refuses to let Favor's
herd drink.

NOTES: Writer John Dunkel wrote twenty scripts for *Rawhide*, by
far the most, and also penned installments of *Bonanza*, *Gunsmoke*,
The Big Valley and *The High Chaparral*. He was eighty-six at the
time of his death in 2001.

Nina Foch and Fleming in "Incident of the Judas Trap."

#20: Incident of the Judas Trap
(June 5, 1959)

DIRECTOR: Jesse Hibbs

WRITER: David Lang

CAST: Nina Foch, Gerald Mohr, Jane Nigh, Phyllis Coates, Hugh Sanders, John Bleifer, Larry Thor, Paul McGuire, Rush Williams, Rick Arnold, Milan Smith

NARRATION: "A human bein' can take a lot of punishment. You find that out real quick when you drive cattle. You head along a thousand miles of dust, you cuss the day that man ever decided to eat beef. We're tryin' to bring it to the market: Sedalia, Missouri. We don't always like what we have to do to get it there. But that's part of my job. My name's Gil Favor, trail boss."

The drive is attacked by wolves, and the river is too high for the cattle to cross. Rowdy finds a line shack filled with wolf traps, guarded by a woman with a gun.

NOTES: Sheb Wooley's biggest role to date as Pete Nolan finds his pre-war girlfriend. Some of the wolves are actually German shepherds. Third episode with a drover named Kyle.

#21: INCIDENT IN NO MAN'S LAND
(JUNE 12, 1959)

DIRECTOR: Jack Arnold
STORY: Lawrence L. Goldman
TELEPLAY: Buckley Angell
CAST: Brian Keith, Phyllis Avery, Reed Hadley, Adam Williams, Mary Beth Hughes, Don Megowan, Shirley Knight, Dee J. Thompson, Ron Foster, Maria Monay, Larry Blake

NARRATION: "Those cows have a right to bellow. On a drive like this they often have to go for days without grass or water. The men drivin' 'em have a right to gripe. Often they have to go without food, water and sleep. I have a right to worry about both, man and beast. That's part of my job. I'm Gil Favor, trail boss."

Explosions are spooking the herd, and when Favor and Rowdy ride off to investigate, they find an encampment filled by women related to convicts using dynamite in the local mine.

NOTES: Shot in the famed Los Angeles quarry known as Bronson Canyon, a location for literally hundreds of television shows and films since the silent era. Brian Keith starred in Sam Peckinpah's short-lived and underrated series *The Westerner*.

#22: INCIDENT OF A BURST OF EVIL
(JUNE 26, 1959)

DIRECTOR: George Sherman
WRITER: Buckley Angell
CAST: Linda Cristal, H.M. Wynant, Elisha Cook, Charles

Bateman, Eve McVeagh, Russ Bender, Kenneth McDonald, Ralph Votrian, Jean Tatum, Ezelle Poule, Dick Nelson

NARRATION: "Pretty hard to beat it when it sets in solid—boredom. You can feel it close in like heat around your riders, watch it dull 'em to the point where the drive gets to be something they'd just as soon forget. But they can't afford to forget it. I can't afford to let 'em. My name's Gil Favor, trail boss."

Mushy claims to have seen a wild man in the hills four times in the past two days, and so do Wishbone, Quince and Scarlett. The man sneaks into camp and warns the drive that Comancheros are going to attack.

NOTES: Good episode with an action-packed finale. Linda Cristal received an Emmy nomination for her portrayal of Victoria Cannon on *The High Chapparal.*

#23: INCIDENT OF THE ROMAN CANDLES
(JULY 10, 1959)

DIRECTOR: Stuart Heisler
WRITER: Jan Winters
CAST: Richard Eyer, Beverly Garland, Bob Ellenstein, Will Wright, Gerald Milton, Zon Murray, Bill Henry, Robert Griffin, William Tannen, David McMahon, Don Wilbanks, Margie Liszt, David Wanger, Tom Wilde

NARRATION: "On a trail drive a man can find the things he wants— a sense of God's good earth, the room to move in, a job to be done. Of course there's not always enough water, and you can't always choose your own company. There's some that say that's all that's wrong with Hell. That's up to me to handle—the good and bad. I'm Gil Favor, trail boss."

Pete finds a young boy walking across the plains with nothing but an armful of Roman candles. Back with the drive, the boy's explanation of his situation keeps changing until no one knows what to believe. Pete soon learns the menacing truth.

Richard Eyer and Sheb Wooley in "Incident of the Roman Candles."

NOTES: First episode to feature Sheb Wooley almost exclusively. Richard Eyer co-starred on the series *Stagecoach West* and appeared with Paul Brinegar in the 1957 film *The Invisible Boy*.

Season Two

#24: Incident of the Day of the Dead
(September 18, 1959)

Director: Stuart Heisler

Writers: David Victor & Herbert Little, Jr.

Cast: Viveca Lindfors, Alexander Scourby, Nancy Hadley, Ron Soble, Charles Romero, Helen Westcott, Hal Baylor, Maurice Jara, Alex Montoya, William Fawcett, Claire Carleton, Connie Buck, Pilar Arcos, Julian Rivero

Narration (by Clint Eastwood): "On a trail drive, each and every man has his chore. The eye of the drive is the scout, riding out in front to test the trail and find water and bed ground. Others are stationed around the herd, hazing it when it moves and soothing it when it's bedded down. A very important man is master of the chuck wagon, because he's not only got to be a good trail cook, but a jack of all trades as well. The man who holds the whole kit and caboodle together is the trail boss. There's one man in the outfit who's got no chores of his own, gotta be ready and willin' to take over anyone else's. Yeah, that's me—ramrod of this outfit, Rowdy Yates."

While waiting to pick up the drive's mail in a trail town, Rowdy impresses the woman owner of a large ranch. He runs up a three hundred dollar debt playing poker and is given a chance to earn the money by breaking a wild horse at the ranch.

Notes: Like the first season, a rather weak premiere, complete with weird Theremin music. Although Rowdy is the only member of the drive present, the episode is more of a showcase for guest star Lindfors.

None of the other regulars are listed in the closing credits, nor is Robert Cabal, who plays a ranch hand rather than Hey-Soos.

#25: INCIDENT AT DANGERFIELD DIP
(OCTOBER 2, 1959)

DIRECTOR: Robert Webb
STORY: Herbert Purdum
TELEPLAY: Fred Freiberger
CAST: Phillip Pine, Alan Baxter, Douglas Kennedy, Bert Remsen, Pitt Herbert, Gregg Barton, Dorothy Morris

NARRATION: "On the trail to Sedalia, Missouri—day to day—you fall into the habit of tryin' to read your men, guess what makes 'em tick. But you don't make much headway. Isn't easy to figure grown-up humans who take this kind of life for thirty bucks a month and keep. So you finally give up. And you're just glad there's a breed like 'em to get the beeves to where they're goin'. I've got a good reason to be glad. My name's Gil Favor, trail boss."

The herd is deliberately infected with Spanish tick fever by men demanding an exorbitant fee to let the drovers run the cattle through the chemical dip that will remedy the situation.

NOTES: Jim Quince and Joe Scarlett are given more to do than usual. A baby's name is changed to James "Wishbone" Kincaid by a grateful father.

#26: INCIDENT OF THE SHAMBLING MAN
(OCTOBER 9, 1959)

DIRECTOR: Andrew V. McLaglen
STORY: Charles Larson
TELEPLAY: Charles Larson & Fred Freiberger
CAST: Victor McLaglen, Anne Francis, Gene Nelson, Robert Lowery, Harry Carey, Jr., Robert Karnes, Earle Hodgins, Stephen Joyce, Ed Faulkner, Steve Thomas, Russell Trent, Pamela Duncan, Ann McCrea, Bruce Wendell

NARRATION: "Cows are senseless, stupid beasts. They go halfway across the continent just to be slaughtered. The trouble is, nobody ever trained 'em to go alone. It takes men to push a herd north. Men and time and sometimes pain. That's where I come in. I'm one of the men. Gil Favor, trail boss."

A heartless woman attempts to have her father-in-law, a former bare-knuckle fighter, committed to an insane asylum so she will not have to take care of him. Favor and Rowdy initially take her side.

NOTES: Final performance in the legendary career of Victor McLaglen (who was directed in this episode by his son Andrew): the elder McLaglen died in November 1959. Ed Faulkner appeared on *Rawhide* seven times.

#27: INCIDENT AT JACOB'S WELL
(OCTOBER 16, 1959)

DIRECTOR: Jack Arnold
WRITER: Robert Sherman
CAST: David Brian, Patricia Medina, Jean Allison, Henry Rowland, Mason Curry, Kathleen O'Malley, Dean Williams

NARRATION: "On a trail drive, you pick your men to be at least as smart as the cows. The cows know enough to drink up when there's water, to stop and eat when there's food. The mean can do that, too, but the rest of their thinking—man or beast—I'm supposed to do for 'em, whether I do it right or not. My name's Gil Favor, trail boss."

A bad drought has forced several farming families to eat their horses to survive. When Favor tells them he cannot spare any of the remuda, the farmers decide to steal the horses under cover of darkness.

NOTES: The main cast is becoming better defined in the second season. A grave marker indicates the year is 1870.

Eastwood.

#28: Incident of the Thirteenth Man
(October 23, 1959)

DIRECTOR: Jesse Hibbs
STORY: Endre Bohem
TELEPLAY: Fred Freiberger
CAST: Edward C. Platt, Richard Shannon, Paul Fix, Jerome Cowan, Terry Becker, Robert Cornthwaite, Russell Thorson, Mike Ragan, Harry Antrim, Iron Eyes Cody, John Hart, Robert Anderson, Grant Richards

NARRATION: None

Rowdy and Wishbone are roped into jury duty when they ride into Blanton, Texas, looking for a dentist to fix Wishbone's ailing tooth. The town is filled with bullies, misfits and cowards—and the trial is anything but above board.

NOTES: Mainly a showcase for several well-known character actors and mostly talk. Paul Fix was co-starring as Marshal Micah Torrence on *The Rifleman* when this episode was shot.

#29: Incident at the Buffalo Smokehouse
(October 30, 1959)

DIRECTOR: Stuart Heisler
STORY: Joseph Vogel
TELEPLAY: Louis Vittes
CAST: Vera Miles, Gene Evans, Leif Erickson, Allison Hayes, John Agar, J. Pat O'Malley, Dean Stanton, Jack Weston, Lane Bradford, Karl Swenson, Harry Swoger, Bob Tetrick, Glenn Turnbull

NARRATION: (Favor shown writing in journal) "The trail log says every workin' cowhand has a string of horses assigned to him. That string's made up of the different kinds he's gonna need. Circle horse, cuttin' horse, a ropin' horse, one or two broncs. He works with 'em, worries over 'em and wouldn't be worth a brass nickel without 'em. Same goes for me, 'cept my string isn't horses—it's men. I'm Gil Favor, trail boss."

Trying to outrun a prairie fire, Favor locates a river that might stop it. He asks a rancher's wife where the best place is for the herd to cross and ends up as one of the hostages of an outlaw gang.

NOTES: One of the most colorful guest casts of the entire series. Gene Evans appeared in six episodes and was given a Golden Boot Award in 1988, ten years before his death at age 75. No "Head 'em up, move 'em out!"

#30: INCIDENT OF THE HAUNTED HILLS
(NOVEMBER 6, 1959)

DIRECTOR: Jesse Hibbs
STORY: Oliver Crawford
TELEPLAY: Louis Vittes
CAST: John Drew Barrymore, Kent Smith, Strother
               Martin, Charles Gray, Marya Stevens, Clarke
               Gordon, Harry Lauter, Ron Hayes, Moody
               Blanchard, John Kroger, Glenn Strange, Bart
               Bradley

NARRATION: "When things are goin' right on a drive, a trail hand will call everything from a calf to a ten-year-old bull a cow. When they're not goin' right, which is most of the time, he'll call cattle lots of other names, very few of them are complimentary. I know 'em all. I'm Gil Favor, trail boss."

With the nearest source of water thirty miles away, Favor realizes the drive's only option is to explore territory known as the Haunted Hills, which is inhabited by an unfriendly Indian tribe.

NOTES: Filmed in an area variously known as Conejo Flats, Conejo Valley or Conejo Ranch. Water for the geyser was supplied by a nearby lake. Second and final guest appearance by Charles Gray before joining the cast in 1961. Glenn Strange later became a member of the *Gunsmoke* family as bartender Sam Noonan, also in 1961.

#31: Incident of the Stalking Death
(November 13, 1959)

Director: Harmon Jones
Story: Oliver Crawford & Louis Vittes
Teleplay: Louis Vittes
Cast: Cesar Romero, Mari Blanchard, Martin Garalaga, Regis Toomey, Scott Davey, Marilyn Winston, Doug Wilson

Narration: "Pushin' a trail drive is like movin' a whole town that isn't sure it wants to be moved. Some of its people are willin'—some aren't. You start out with problems, then you meet up with new ones. Whatever they are, however they happen, they have to be met. That's my job. Gil Favor's my name, trail boss.

Favor's arm is badly gashed by a puma that has been attacking the herd. The grandfather of a boy killed by the wild cat helps the drovers track the animal down.

Notes: Ranch set the same one used in "Incident of the Roman Candles." Wishbone reveals that he was once a mountain man. Favor mentions his having two daughters and that his wife is dead. First of Cesar Romero's four episodes of *Rawhide*.

#32: Incident of the Valley in the Shadow
(November 20, 1959)

Director: Harmon Jones
Writer: Buckley Angell
Cast: Rick Jason, Fay Spain, Leo Gordon, Arthur Batanides, John Cole, Don Harvey, John Erwin

Narration: "There's money in beef, but it doesn't come easy. There's a market for all the steers you can raise. But it's a thousand miles away. You get top prices only for top cattle. Pushin' the herd up the trail is only half the job. You've gotta get it there in good shape. It takes tough men workin' long hours for low wages, starin' trouble in the face at every bend in the trail. I'm one of 'em. Gil Favor, trail boss."

Favor hires a pair of bounty hunters to help with the herd, unaware that the men are really searching for a girl abducted by the Cheyenne, or that Pete holds a grudge against one of them.

NOTES: New opening, with cattle shown crossing a river. (There were several openings, not only for each season, but also within seasons.) Semi-regular Collins (Don Harvey) says his family was killed by the Cheyenne when the drive reaches the ruins of a ranch house. Rick Jason's second *Rawhide* appearance. Leo Gordon also made two episodes and was given a Golden Boot Award in 1997.

#33: INCIDENT OF THE BLUE FIRE
(DECEMBER 11, 1959)

DIRECTOR: Charles Marquis Warren
WRITER: John Dunkel
CAST: Skip Homeier, Robert Cabal, Joe De Santis, Don Harvey, John Erwin

NARRATION: "Old timers always say, 'It doesn't storm like it used to.' But I'll argue with 'em. When you're on a trail drive, you get on intimate terms with the weather. You're away from home maybe eight, nine months, and you may not sleep under a roof the whole time. Rain, sleet, snow—whatever it has to offer, it's part of the job, my job. Gil Favor's the name, trail boss."

With an electrical storm looming, both the cattle and the drovers are feeling spooked. Not helping matters are superstitious tales told by Hey-Soos, the arrival of a stranger and a particularly troublesome steer.

NOTES: First episode with Robert Cabal as Hey-Soos since episode eighteen.

#34: INCIDENT AT SPANISH ROCK
(DECEMBER 18, 1959)

WRITER: Harmon Jones
STORY: Claire Huffaker
TELEPLAY: Louis Vittes
CAST: Elena Verdugo, Jacques Aubuchon, Frank DeKova, Wolfe Barzell, Pepe Hern, Roberto Contreras, Jorge Moreno, Vincent Padula, George Ramsey

NARRATION: None

Mexican soldiers order Favor to turn over one of the drovers, allegedly the son of the man leading a rebellion against President Diaz.

NOTES: Ranch location the same as "Incident of the Dry Drive." Roberto Contreras later portrayed ranch hand Pedro on the first three seasons of *The High Chaparral.*

#35: INCIDENT OF THE DRUID CURSE (JANUARY 8, 1960)

DIRECTOR: Jesse Hibbs
STORY: Alva Hudson
TELEPLAY: Louis Vittes
CAST: Claude Akins, Luana Patten, Byron Foulger, Don Keefer, Stanley Adams

NARRATION: "When it comes to cattle you can brand 'em with a bar brand, a bench brand, or a bosell brand, which is a stripe runnin' around the cow's nose. Or you can use a runnin' or a swingin' brand, a tumblin' or a walkin' brand, whose lower part looks like feet. But whichever you use, from then on, you know who the cow belongs to. When it comes to men, though, it's not that easy. They don't wear brands. What herd they're runnin' with, what loyalties they got, is anybody's guess. And I can't afford to guess. I'm Gil Favor, trail boss."

The drive comes across an archaeologist and his daughter who are searching for remnants of a pagan civilization with roots in ancient England. Outlaws, believing the pair is looking for valuable treasure, take them captive.

NOTES: Like "Incident of the Day of the Dead" and "Incident of the Blue Fire," another eerie episode. Gil Favor's first kiss of the series. Claude Akins made seven episodes of *Rawhide*, more than any other major guest star. He died in 1994 at age 75.

#36: INCIDENT AT RED RIVER STATION
(JANUARY 12, 1960)

DIRECTOR: Gene Fowler, Jr.

WRITER: Charles Larson

CAST: James Dunn, Robert F. Simon, Stanley Clements, William Tanner, Glen Gordon, Peter Adams, Frances Morris, Earl Hansen, Earle Hodgins, Kim Hector, Dorothy Christmas

NARRATION: None

Threatened by an epidemic of smallpox, Favor ends up assisting a doctor whose cure is opposed by a skeptical community.

NOTES: James Dunn won an Academy Award in 1945 for *A Tree Grows in Brooklyn*. The voice of child actor Kim Hector was dubbed by actress June Foray, also the voice of Rocky J. Squirrel on *The Bullwinkle Show*. Coincidentally, her voice was substituted for Mary Badham's in an episode of *The Twilight Zone* whose cast included Kim Hector.

#37: INCIDENT OF THE DEVIL AND HIS DUE
(JANUARY 22, 1960)

DIRECTOR: Harmon Jones

WRITERS: Samuel Newman & Louis Vittes

CAST: Neville Brand, Louis Jean Heydt, John Pickard, Sheila Bromley, James Griffith, Ralph Reed, Peter Mamakos, Ken Mayer, Hank Worden, Barbara Morrison, Fred E. Sherman, Hal Taggart

NARRATION: "The cowhand's hat is the first thing he puts on when he gets up. And the last thing he takes off when he beds down. Some of the wide brim shades his eyes from the sun. In winter, he pulls the brim down, ties it over his ears to avoid frostbite. Uses the crown as a bucket and the brim as a drinkin' cup. That's why a cowhand'll get the best hat he can. 'Cause it's got to serve a dozen purposes its maker never dreamed of. The same thing goes for the men wearin' the hats. I know. I'm Gil Favor, trail boss."

Favor scouts for a way around a rockslide that has stalled the herd, only to find a rancher who has been shot to death. The trail boss is arrested for the murder, and the local sheriff deputizes Rowdy.

NOTES: A solid entry featuring the first of Neville Brand's two *Rawhide* performances. John Pickard made a total of ten episodes. Hank Worden, a member of director John Ford's acting company, is best remembered for his role in *The Searchers*.

#38: INCIDENT OF THE WANTED PAINTER (JANUARY 29, 1960)

DIRECTOR: Harmon Jones
WRITER: Charles Larson
CAST: Arthur Franz, Steve Brodie, Robert Lowery, Dennis Cross, Charles Maxwell, Frank Wolff, Rex Holman, Norman Winston

NARRATION: None

Favor learns that Major Sinclair, the officer he served under during the Civil War, has been framed for murder and is about to be hanged.

NOTES: Fleming sounds as if he has a cold. Rowdy once again mentions his having been a prisoner of war. Second appearance by Robert Lowery, who starred as Big Tim Champion in the adventure series *Circus Boy*.

#39: INCIDENT OF THE TINKER'S DAM (FEBRUARY 5, 1960)

DIRECTOR: Gene Fowler, Jr.
WRITER: Jan Winters
CAST: Regis Toomey, Anthony Dexter, Ron Soble, Herbert Patterson, Robert Chadwick, Jeanne Bates, Ray Montgomery, Monte Blue, Iron Eyes Cody, Russ Conklin, Estelita Zarco

NARRATION: "It takes three things to make a trail drive: cattle, horses and men. And some say two because a man without a horse is no man at all. There are mornin's when I think a horse without a man would be better. I should know men by now, but I keep learnin'. I'm Gil Favor, trail boss."

Wishbone's twin brother, Thomas Jefferson Wishbone, rides into camp with a band of Indians in pursuit. The drovers stage a phony burial service to convince the Indians that T.J. is dead.

NOTES: Wishbone and T.J. refer to each other as "little brother." Mushy's first chance at an action sequence, though he faints afterward. The name of Brinegar's character in the film *Cattle Empire* was Thomas Jefferson. Fleming sounds as if he is still suffering from a cold. Regis Toomey played a different character in "Incident of the Stalking Death."

#40: INCIDENT OF THE NIGHT HORSE
(FEBRUARY 19, 1960)

DIRECTOR: Joe Kane
WRITER: John Dunkel
CAST: George Wallace, Judy Nugent, Madeleine Holmes, John Erwin
NARRATION: None
Several cattle are corralled in a mustang trap set by a rancher determined to catch the wild horse that killed his son. In the past, the rancher killed one of Favor's friends.

NOTES: Fleming and guest star Wallace engage in one of the best knock down, drag out fights of the series.

#41: INCIDENT OF THE SHARPSHOOTER
(FEBRUARY 26, 1960)

DIRECTOR: Jesse Hibbs
WRITER: Winston Miller
CAST: Jock Mahoney, Hugh Sanders, Stafford Repp, Raymond Greenleaf, Harry Ellerbe, Morgan Jones, Norman Leavitt, Olan Soule, Kenne Duncan, John Hart, Harold Goodwin, Fred Lerner, Casey McGregor, George Hickman, Terry Loomis

Eastwood and Fleming.

NARRATION: None

Rowdy is suspected of a murder actually committed by a gunman pretending to be an attorney.

NOTES: At one point Favor wears a checkered shirt rather than his usual dusty trail attire. In addition to being an accomplished stunt man, Jock Mahoney starred in the syndicated series *The Range Rider* and was a latter day Tarzan. This was the first his two *Rawhide* episodes. He died in 1989.

#42: INCIDENT OF THE DUST FLOWER
(MARCH 4, 1960)

DIRECTOR: Ted Post
WRITER: Winston Miller
CAST: Margaret Phillips, Arthur Shields, Tom Drake, Frances Bavier, Doreen Lang, John Cole, Len Hendry, Fern Berry, Don Happy

NARRATION: "It sounds simple when you start out: Get the herd to Abilene. Before you're halfway there, the cattle are the least of your worries. I know. Gil Favor, trail boss.

Pete comes to the aid of a timid woman perceived as a spinster, sparing her embarrassment at his own expense.

NOTES: A gentle, rather poignant story and one of Wooley's more effective performances. Tom Drake was one of the stars of the classic musical drama *Meet Me in St. Louis* (1944). Frances Bavier will always be remembered as the beloved Aunt Bee on *The Andy Griffith Show*.

#43: INCIDENT AT SULPHUR CREEK
(MARCH 11, 1960)

DIRECTOR: Harmon Jones
STORY: Sloan Nibley
TELEPLAY: Louis Vittes
CAST: John Dehner, Jan Shepard, Charles Aidman, Ross Ford, Howard Wendell, Robert Cabal, James Gavin, Duane Grey, K.L. Smith, Joseph Vitale, X Brands, William R. Thompkins, Jr.

NARRATION: None

The drive has to contend with Comanches, horse thieves and a woman in love with her husband's brother.

NOTES: A highlight of the second season, thanks largely to solid performances by Dehner, who made five guest appearances, and Jan Shepard, who made three. Robert Cabal's third episode as horse wrangler Hey-Soos. William Thompkins, a friend of Clint Eastwood, would later join the series as semi-regular "Toothless" Jeffries.

#44: Incident of the Champagne Bottles
(March 18, 1960)

DIRECTOR: Joe Kane
STORY: Curtis Kenyon
TELEPLAY: Louis Vittes
CAST: Hugh Marlowe, Patricia Barry, Lane Bradford, John Hart

NARRATION: None

The drive comes across a rider and a couple driving a wagon loaded with two dozen cases of imported champagne, unaware that some of the bottles contain nitroglycerin.

NOTES: Lane Bradford, usually cast as a heavy, made five episodes of *Rawhide*, nowhere near as many as John Hart, who made seventeen. Patricia Barry, who appeared twice, was a familiar face to Western fans, guest starring on more than twenty series.

#45: Incident of the Stargazer
(April 1, 1960)

DIRECTOR: Harmon Jones
STORY: Jan Winters & Ted Gardner
TELEPLAY: Louis Vittes
CAST: Buddy Ebsen, Dorothy Green, Richard Webb, Ted de Corsia, Jonathan Hole, Marya Stevens, Tom Fadden, Kelton Garwood, Clem Fuller

NARRATION: None

Pete sees a stagecoach drop a woman off with no homestead or town in sight. She has come from Philadelphia to join her husband, an astronomer. But when she tells Pete the man who claims to be her husband is an imposter, the man says she is mentally ill.

NOTES: No sign of Rowdy. Ranch house is the same one used in "Incident at Jacob's Well." Dorothy Green would later portray Gil Favor's sister-in-law in two episodes. Buddy Ebsen, who went on to star in *The Beverly Hillbillies* and *Barnaby Jones*, first portrayed Fess Parker's sidekick in Disney's *Davy Crockett*.

#46: INCIDENT OF THE DANCING DEATH
(APRIL 8, 1960)

DIRECTOR: William Claxton
STORY: Dallas Gaultois & James Edmiston
TELEPLAY: Buckley Angell
CAST: Mabel Albertson, Kipp Hamilton, Anthony Caruso, Paul Picerni, Robert Cabal, Warren Oates, Michael Mark, Bill Talbot, William R. Thompkins, John Cole

NARRATION: "Only thing certain about a trail drive is the uncertainty. The expected never seems to happen. The surprise is always popping up, most of the time bringin' trouble. When it hits there's no countin' on somebody else to handle it. That's my job, mine alone. I'm Gil Favor, trail boss."

A gypsy steals Favor's best horse, and while Favor and Rowdy give chase, a gypsy girl avoiding an arranged marriage pops out of Wishbone's wagon. Favor's horse returns on its own, the thief stabbed to death.

NOTES: Robert Cabal still not listed with the regular cast. The performances by the legendary Warren Oates, who would guest star in three more episodes, is unfortunately brief. Music, by Leith Stevens, is given a separate on-screen credit. Some musical cues and motifs in this episode and others are from the MGM library and can be heard in the 1962 epic *How the West Was Won*.

#47: INCIDENT OF THE ARANA SACAR
(APRIL 22, 1960)

DIRECTOR: Joe Kane
STORY: Charles Marquis Warren
TELEPLAY: Buckley Angell
CAST: Cloris Leachman, Russell Arms, Chris Alcaide, Hal Baylor, Charles Fredericks

NARRATION (OVER SHOT OF JOE SCARLETT): "This is a drover. He's tough and he's durable. He has to match his strength and skill against the orneriness of cattle. Normally he's steady goin' and dependable, 'cept once in a while, when the orneriness of the cattle rubs off on him. Then I've got a problem, and it's usually a bad one. My name's Gil Favor, trail boss."

With the drovers getting testy, they head off for a nearby trading post to blow off steam. While gone, a gang of hide skinners steals the herd.

NOTES: Sheb Wooley sings "Bury Me Not on the Lone Prairie" to soothe the cattle. Wishbone and Mushy watch Joe and Jim fight, and when Pete pulls them apart, they walk away as though nothing ever happened. Well-known Western bad man Chris Alcaide, who was in four episodes, won a Golden Boot Award in 2003, one year before his death at age eighty-one. Hal Baylor, in nine episodes, died in 1998, age eighty.

#48: INCIDENT OF THE DESERTER
(APRIL 29, 1960)

DIRECTOR: Gerd Oswald
STORY: Buckley Angell, Jessica Benson & Louis Vittes
TELEPLAY: Louis Vittes

NARRATION (BY PAUL BRINEGAR): "The way I heard it, it was some French fella named Napoleon said an army marches on its belly. Well, I don't know much about armies, but I mighty well know that's true about trail drives. The beeves eat what they can, but the drovers are a little more particular. So one day I'll cook 'em pig vests with buttons—that's salt pork and beans. Next day they'll get Kansas City fish—that's salt pork with brown berries, and that's beans. The day after that they're liable to get sow belly. That's salt pork. This time with prairie strawberries. And that's beans. So the fourth day I stay out of sight. My name's Wishbone, feeder of the Gil Favor outfit."

Tired of the drudgery of cooking, as well as hearing the men complain about the quality of the cuisine, Wishbone figures it might be time to settle down. In Iron City, he winds up with his own restaurant—and a potential bride.

NOTES: An amusing change of pace episode in which Wishbone gets the stove seen in later installments. Fleming and Eastwood billed in separate titles in the closing credits. Another episode without Rowdy.

#49: INCIDENT OF THE ONE HUNDRED AMULETS
(MAY 6, 1960)

DIRECTOR: Stuart Heisler
STORY: Fred Freiberger & Lawrence Menkin
TELEPLAY: Fred Freiberger & Louis Vittes
CAST: R.G. Armstrong, Whit Bissel, Vaughn Taylor, Robert Cabal, Argentina Brunetti, Virginia Christine, Richard Reeves, Pat Michon, Ed Nelson, Carol Sellinger, John Erwin, Alex Montoya, Peter Whitney

NARRATION: None
Favor tells Hey-Soos he can go into town to recuperate from an injury and visit his mother, Rosa Patines. When he asks where her ranch is located, he is stoned by a mob.

NOTES: Robert Cabal's first substantial episode, though still billed with the guest cast. Fleming and Eastwood are back on the same title card in the end credits.

#50: INCIDENT OF THE MURDER STEER
(MAY 13, 1960)

DIRECTOR: Joe Kane
WRITER: John Dunkel
CAST: James Franciscus, Whitney Blake, Howard Petrie, Paul Lukather, Robert Cabal, John Erwin, Robert Jordan, Stephen Joyce

NARRATION: "In those eastern newspapers they write about the lawlessness of the West. But they don't know what it really means to live that way. It means in time of trouble you've got no help but the quickness of your own right hand. No judge but your own good sense, especially on trail herd. Most of the time you're one hundred miles from anyone wearin' a lawman's star. So keepin' order is up to me. Name's Gil Favor, trail boss."

Soon after Favor hires four new drovers from the same town, murders start occurring, accompanied by sightings of a cow with the word "murder" painted on its side. Favor and Hey-Soos say the murder steer is an old legend, but Rowdy says he has seen it.

NOTES: A sometimes confusing episode with an unexpected ending. Another superstitious storyline automatically requiring the presence of Hey-Soos. Fleming and Eastwood are once again billed separately.

#51: INCIDENT OF THE MUSIC MAKER
(MAY 20, 1960)

DIRECTOR: R.G. Springsteen
STORY: Rick Vollaerts
TELEPLAY: Charles Larson
CAST: Peter Whitney, Lili Kardell, Werner Klemperer, Robert Boon, Jerry Barclay, Norman Winston, John Durren, Robert Griffin, Ted Stanhope, John Cole, Bob Duggan, X Brands
NARRATION: None

Favor and Rowdy stop to let their horses drink "lukewarm mud" and hear a music box playing Beethoven's "Minuet in G." They find an immigrant gunsmith burying his wife and invite him to join the drive, not knowing he plans to steal part of the herd.

NOTES: Burly Peter Whitney, who had just appeared in the episode "Incident of the One Hundred Amulets," guest starred on more than forty Western series and co-starred in ABC's *The Rough Riders*.

#52: INCIDENT OF THE SILENT WEB
(JUNE 3, 1960)

DIRECTOR: Joe Kane
WRITERS: Winston Miller & Charles B. Smith
CAST: Reba Waters, Don Haggerty, William Thourlby, Charles Maxwell, Paul Langton, Carlos Romero, Joseph Patridge, Pat O'Moore, Stephen Ellsworth, John War Eagle

NARRATION: None

The drive takes in a mute little girl and her father, who says they were attacked by escaped convicts, but the drovers question his story.

NOTES: Rowdy in charge, Favor said to be up ahead buying the drive's right-of-way through the territory. Wishbone makes popcorn in the stove he acquired in "Incident of the Deserter." Same isolated two-story ranch house used in "Incident at Jacob's Well" and "Incident of the Stargazer." Rowdy says "Head 'em up, move 'em out!" Fleming and Eastwood credited at the beginning of the episode for the first time. Sheb Wooley and Paul Brinegar have separate credits at the end, with James Murdock, Steve Raines and Rocky Shahan on the same title card in larger print than before.

#53: INCIDENT OF THE LAST CHANCE
(JUNE 10, 1960)

DIRECTOR: Ted Post
WRITER: Winston Miller
CAST: John Kerr, Roxanne Berard, John Marley, Kathryn
              Card, Jon Lormer, Dick Elliott, William D. Gordon,
              Hank Patterson, Bob Hopkins, Guy Teague

NARRATION: None

On the way to a ranch owned by Hank Eaton, the drive is joined by Eaton's nephew Bert and his new bride, both inexperienced in the ways of the West.

NOTES: Lighthearted episode, an almost trivial episode, yet entertaining. One of the first to open with guest stars rather than the regular cast. Rowdy says his father once advised him to stay away from married women the same time he gave him his first razor.

#54: INCIDENT IN THE GARDEN OF EDEN
(JUNE 17, 1960)

DIRECTOR: Joe Kane
STORY: Irwin & Gwen Gielgud
TELEPLAY: Louis Vittes

CAST: John Ireland, Debra Paget, Robert Coote, John Hoyt, J. Pat O'Malley, Pat O'Moore, Gregory Walcott, Adrienne Marden, Charles Davis, Joan Elan, John Cole

Rowdy offers to buy some cattle from a British rancher who will not sell, but his daughter disagrees. The ranch's foreman orders Rowdy to pack up and leave.

NOTES: Like the season opener, the second season concludes with a show centered exclusively around Eastwood. Wishbone gives the order to "Head 'em up, move 'em out!" John Ireland would become a regular cast member in the final season. The first of Gregory Walcott's five episodes. John Cole, usually drover Bailey, plays an Indian. Debra Paget co-starred in the big screen Westerns *Broken Arrow* and *Love Me Tender.*

SEASON THREE

#55: INCIDENT AT ROJO CANYON
(SEPTEMBER 30, 1960)

DIRECTOR: Ted Post
WRITERS: Budd Bankson & Steve Raines
CAST: Julie London, Bobby Troup, Frank Maxwell, John Pickard, Stanley Clements, Bill Wellman, Jr., Nelson Welch, Robert Easton, Richard Gering, Tom Troupe, Linden Chiles, Len Hendry

NARRATION: None

The drive crosses paths with Anne Danvers, a singer searching for her father, and a small army of renegade Confederate soldiers who do not know the war is over.

NOTES: Jim Quince and Joe Scarlett have larger roles than ever before, thanks no doubt to Steve Raines being co-writer of the story. Fleming and Eastwood are credited at the beginning and the end of the episode. Endre Bohem is credited as both story consultant and associate producer. Julie London (who sings "Perfect Love") and Bobby Troup were, at the time, real life man and wife.

#56: INCIDENT OF THE CHALLENGE
(OCTOBER 14, 1960)

DIRECTOR: Charles Marquis Warren
STORY: Charles Marquis Warren
TELEPLAY: Charles Larson
CAST: Lyle Bettger, Michael Pate, Robert Cabal, Ann Doran, Orville Sherman, John Hart,

Fleming and Julie London in "Incident at Rojo Canyon."

Harry Ellerbe, Vici Raaf, John Erwin, John Cole
NARRATION: "On the Sedalia Trail the weather's like a Texas woman: contrary and full of little tricks to keep a man off balance. No use tryin' to outguess either one of 'em. If they give you trouble, all you can do is pray for a change, hope for the best. I've had a passing acquaintance with both. Name's Gil Favor, trail boss."

Running from a tornado, Favor's horse stumbles and throws him. When the trail boss comes to, an old Aztec named Mitla gives him water. Hey-Soos says Mitla is looking for his daughter, a holy woman who supposedly has magical powers.

NOTES: The year is said to be 1869, contradicting earlier episodes. The second of Michael Pate's five appearances. John Cole once again plays an Indian rather than drover Bailey.

#57: INCIDENT AT DRAGOON CROSSING
(OCTOBER 21, 1960)

DIRECTOR: Ted Post
WRITER: John Dunkel
CAST: Dan O'Herlihy, Duane Grey, Gary Walberg,
              Ralph Thomas, John Erwin

NARRATION: "Takin' a herd north you have to trail across nearly a thousand miles of the wrinkled skin of earth. Over terrain as strange and different as paradise above from the hot place below. Mostly it's too rough or too steep, too wet or dry, too hot or cold, too windy, too lonely. But you takes what comes and find a way to move the beeves on through. At least you try. My name's Gil Favor, trail boss."

Rowdy is upset when Favor becomes ill and entrusts the herd to another trail boss instead of him, especially when the other boss is suspected of being in cahoots with outlaws charging a toll to let the herd cross a river.

NOTES: Favor reveals he is sometimes bothered by a skull fracture he received in the war, and says he might quit some day and go back East. Garry Walberg appeared as a drover in several episodes but was only given on-screen credit three times.

#58: INCIDENT OF THE NIGHT VISITOR
(NOVEMBER 4, 1960)

DIRECTOR: R.G. Springsteen
WRITER: John Dunkel
CAST: Dane Clark, Harold J. Stone, Tommy Nolan,
              Robert Cabal, John Erwin, John Cole, Mark
              Norton

NARRATION: "Whenever you hear a fella tellin' about how he rode with a trail herd of five, ten thousand steers, you can call him a liar. The most any crew can handle and keep safe is about three thousand—the size of this herd. With the hazards of weather, terrain, stampedes and Indian raids, that's plenty. Then there's the remuda, the extra horses. That's maybe the most valuable part of the herd, and the most vulnerable. Put that many animals together, they spell trouble. And it's my trouble. Gil Favor's the name, trail boss."

A young boy looking for his father sneaks into camp to look at the faces of the sleeping drovers, including one who could be working with a former outlaw out to steal the remuda.

NOTES: Opening credits feature shots of the seven principle regulars. Tommy Nolan co-starred on the NBC Western *Buckskin*. In addition to two episodes of *Rawhide*, prolific character actor Harold J. Stone guest starred on more than thirty other Western series. Stone died on November 8, 2005, age 92.

#59: INCIDENT OF THE SLAVEMASTER
(NOVEMBER 11, 1960)

DIRECTOR: Ted Post
STORY: Clayton Fox
TELEPLAY: Louis Vittes
CAST: Peter Lorre, John Agar, Lisa Gaye, Theodore
              Newton, Ernest Sarracino, K.T. Stevens, Roy
              Glenn, Steven Courtleigh, Andy Albin, James
              Gavin, John Erwin

NARRATION: "Dependin' on where you come from, you call steers brush splitters, cactus boomers, critters, rawhides, scalawags or baccas. The drovers whose job it is to get 'em where they're goin' call 'em beeves. I'm one of those drovers. We've been pushin' this herd for almost five hundred miles, and it's still nearly twice that to Sedalia, Missouri. My name's Gil Favor, trail boss."

Favor and Pete become unwilling guests of Victor Laurier, a deranged Southerner who has kept former Union soldiers imprisoned ever since the end of the war.

NOTES: Partially filmed in Hollywood's Bronson Canyon, same location used for "Incident in No Man's Land." "Incident of the Slavemaster" is one of only of two television Westerns in the resume of veteran character actor Peter Lorre, who guest starred on *Wagon Train* earlier in 1960.

#60: INCIDENT ON THE ROAD TO YESTERDAY
(NOVEMBER 18, 1960)

DIRECTOR: R.G. Springsteen
WRITERS: Jan Winters & Winston Miller
CAST: Frankie Laine, Chester Morris, Robert Gist, Nan Gray Laine, King Calder, Stephen Joyce, Shirley O'Hara, Charles Tannen, John Erwin, John Cole, George Hickman

NARRATION: None

Ralph Bartlet, a former stage robber who once stole from Favor, sneaks into camp and steals a horse. When Favor and Rowdy catch up to him, he claims he intends to repay all his past victims.

NOTES: Wishbone says he knew all along that there was hope for Ralph, but that "I'm not one for crowin'." Favor smiles and says, "That will be the day." Frankie Laine, singer of the famous *Rawhide* theme, was married to actress Nan Gray Laine.

#61: INCIDENT AT SUPERSTITION PRAIRIE
(DECEMBER 2, 1960)

DIRECTOR: Stuart Heisler
WRITER: Wilton Schiller
CAST: Rudolph Acosta, Michael Pate, Carlos Romero, John Erwin, Robert Cabal, John Cole, Connie Buck

NARRATION: None

Comanches vow to kill all the drovers unless they can restore water to a dry river.

NOTES: No Rowdy in this episode. Rudolph Acosta, usually billed as Rodolfo, portrayed Vaquero on *The High Chapparal*, appeared in more than twenty television Westerns, including four episodes of *Rawhide*.

#62: INCIDENT AT POCO TIEMPO
(DECEMBER 9, 1960)

DIRECTOR: Ted Post
WRITER: Buckley Angell
CAST: Agnes Moorehead, Gigi Perreau, Stewart Bradley,
             Carolyn Hughes, Gregory Walcott, Frank Puglia,
             Lew Gallo, Wally Cassell, Ken Mayer, Allan Nixon,
             Henry Wills, Robert Swan, Bill Hale, John Cason,
             Geoffrey Becton

NARRATION: None

Rowdy and Jim are accused of murdering a priest whom outlaws are holding captive in the church cellar along with two nuns.

NOTES: Rowdy says his father knew the family of one of the nuns. He also reveals he joined the Confederate army at the age of sixteen. Actresses Moorehead and Perreau both appeared in several television Westerns.

#63: INCIDENT OF THE CAPTIVE
(DECEMBER 16, 1960)

DIRECTOR: Stuart Heisler
WRITER: Ted Gardner
CAST: Mercedes McCambridge, Albert Salmi, Bill
             Driscoll, Joe De Santis, Dan Sheridan, Russ
             Bender, Allen Jaffe, Kathryn Card, George
             Johnson, Vic Perrin, Hank Worden, Len Hendry,
             Bud Osborne

NARRATION (BY HARKNESS "MUSHY" MUSHGROVE): "I always thought a trail drive would be an excitin' life, full of adventures. Well, maybe it will be when I'm a real drover. But right now I don't seem to be too important. All my adventures are peelin' potatoes and carryin' water and washin' pots and pans and itchin' Mister Wishbone's back when it scratches. Why, I'm the cook's louse for Mister Favor's trail drive. The men call me Mushy because, well, I guess maybe because it's my name."

Pete suggests staging a phony abduction of Mushy's mother so her son can come to the "rescue" and convince her that he belongs with the drive and not running the family barber shop. No one knows that some real outlaws are after her.

NOTES: The drovers learn that Mushy's real name is Harkness Mushgrove III, and that he cannot read. More location filming at Bronson Canyon. Mercedes McCambridge, who earned a Best Supporting Actress Oscar for 1955's *All the King's Men*, made four episodes of *Rawhide*, but only one as Martha Mushgrove.

#64: INCIDENT OF THE BUFFALO SOLDIER
(JANUARY 1, 1961)

DIRECTOR: Ted Post
WRITER: John Dunkel
CAST: Woody Strode, Ray Montgomery, Roy Glenn, Rupert Crosse, Charles Stevens

NARRATION: None
Rowdy tangles with a hot-headed black soldier who has stabbed a corporal in self defense and is on the run.

NOTES: Fleming and Eastwood again receive billing at both the beginning and end of the episode. Progressive story for its time, with black actors in both lead and supporting roles. Woody Strode was a professional athlete (football, wrestling) and began making films in 1941. His favorite was John Ford's *Sergeant Rutledge* (1960).

#65: INCIDENT OF THE BROKEN WORD
(JANUARY 20, 1961)

DIRECTOR: R.G. Springsteen
WRITER: Louis Vittes
CAST: E.G. Marshall, Dick York, Gloria Talbott, Morris Ankrum, Howard Petrie, Don Diamond, Robert Cabal, Frank Gerstle, John Hart

NARRATION: None
A desperate rancher offers to sell Favor a herd that has contracted anthrax.

NOTES: Once more, a grave marker states the year is 1869. Don Diamond has no dialogue but gets screen credit anyway. Robert Cabal is listed with the cast even though he appears for only a few seconds in a group shot.

#66: INCIDENT AT THE TOP OF THE WORLD
(JANUARY 27, 1961)

DIRECTOR:	Ted Post
STORY:	Peggy & Lou Shaw
TELEPLAY:	Louis Vittes, Peggy & Lou Shaw
CAST:	Robert Culp, Les Tremayne, Jan Shepard, Paul Carr, Ronald Foster, Bill Cutter

Crossing Kansas during cold weather, the drive is met by an army doctor who wants Favor to hire a morphine addicted soldier who was once an experienced drover.

NOTES: One of the most popular episodes of the third season, with another affecting performance by Jan Shepard. Robert Culp starred in his own Western series, *Trackdown*, for two seasons.

#67: INCIDENT NEAR THE PROMISED LAND
(FEBRUARY 3, 1961)

DIRECTOR:	Ted Post
STORY:	Wilton Schiller
TELEPLAY:	John Dunkel
CAST:	Mary Astor, Hugh Sanders, Stafford Repp, Frank Wilcox, Robert Cabal, Don Harvey, John Erwin, John Harmon, Bert Remsen, Michael Ford, Gene Benton

The Gil Favor outfit finally nears Sedalia, only to discover no one is buying cattle. The largest bank in New York has failed, throwing the market into a panic. While Favor looks for grazing land to rent, Wishbone decides to take matters into his own hands.

NOTES: An interesting episode featuring a rare television appearance by screen legend Mary Astor, best known for the 1941 classic

The Maltese Falcon. Bert Remsen played a drover in at least four episodes.

#68: INCIDENT OF THE BIG BLOWOUT
(FEBRUARY 10, 1961)

DIRECTOR: George B. Templeton
WRITER: John Dunkel
CAST: Mari Blanchard, Hugh Sanders, Myron Healey,
             William Tannen, Don Harvey, Dabbs Greer, Frank
             Cady, Robert Cabal, Bert Remsen, John Erwin,
             John Alvin, Ted Stanhope, Curt Barrett, Nick
             Raap, Joe Vitale, Marlene Manners, Len Hendry,
             George Hickman, Tommy Lee
NARRATION: None

In Sedalia, the drovers load the herd into train cars for the army before hitting the town, telling Favor they have had it with cattle driving. Another trail boss asks Favor to go into the cattle raising business with him, and Rowdy is jailed for allegedly shooting a bounty hunter.

NOTES: One of the most enjoyable episodes of the series. The end credits play over a shot of Sedalia's main street. Favor tells Pete he is going to Philadelphia to see his daughters, the drovers refuse to do business with a bigoted storekeeper who will not sell Hey-Soos a shirt, and most of the outfit gets duded up for a photographer. Favor tells everyone the next drive starts in San Antonio in four weeks if any of them are interested.

#69: INCIDENT OF THE FISH OUT OF WATER
(FEBRUARY 17, 1961)

DIRECTOR: Ted Post
WRITER: Albert Aley
CAST: Dorothy Green, George Wallace, Jock Gaynor,
             Candy Moore, Barbara Beaird, Robert Cabal, Fred
             Graham, Max Mellinger
NARRATION: None

Fleming and Candy Moore in "Incident of the Fish Out of Water."

Favor takes a train to Philadelphia to visit his two daughters and sister-in-law who he has not seen in two years. Another passenger is a Pawnee joining a Wild West show to make money for his impoverished tribe, to his eventual regret.

Notes: Favor's sister-in-law tells him he has to decide if he wants to be a drover or a father. Pete and Wishbone show up to see if he is in any kind of trouble. No cattle in the opening credits; drovers shown moving the remuda. Favor's daughter Maggie delivers the famous "Head 'em up, move 'em out!" command to a coach driver at the conclusion of the episode. Shot extensively on MGM's turn of the century street, featured prominently in such classic films as *Meet Me in St. Louis* and television series *The Twilight Zone* and *The*

Outer Limits. Writer Albert Aley was later the story consultant for the CBS series *Cimarron Strip.*

#70: INCIDENT ON THE ROAD BACK
(FEBRUARY 24, 1961)

DIRECTOR: George B. Templeton
WRITER: Louis Vittes
CAST: Gene Evans, Arch Johnson, Jeanne Cooper, Lane Bradford, Brian Hutton, Adrienne Hayes, Mark Tapscott, Dick Elliott, Larry Kent, Len Hendry, Richard Wolf, Jr.

Favor is reunited with his men in Sedalia, but before they can head down to San Antonio, the trail boss is accused of horse stealing.

NOTES: Favor says Pete has quit and is still in Philadelphia. Mushy learns to read from a young woman teacher who gives him a couple of elementary school books to take on the drive.

#71: INCIDENT OF THE NEW START
(MARCH 3, 1961)

DIRECTOR: Justus Addis
STORY: Endre Bohem
TELEPLAY: Charles Larson
CAST: John Dehner, Burt Douglas, Jan Harrison, William Erwin, John Erwin, Robert Bice, Robert Williams, John Hart, Henry Wills, Bill Cutter

NARRATION: None

As the drovers prepare for the next drive from San Antonio to Sedalia, the local cattleman's association replaces Favor with another trail boss who is getting older and wants to participate in one last drive.

NOTES: Pete returns but says he is only passing through on his way to California. Another opening with horses rather than cattle, and legend on the screen: San Antonio, Texas.

#72: Incident of the Running Iron
(March 10, 1961)

Director:	Harmon Jones
Writer:	John Dunkel
Cast:	Darryl Hickman, Addison Richards, John Litel, Frank Wilcox, William Schallert, Kenneth MacDonald, John Erwin, William Thompkins, Thomas F. Martin, William Foster, John Cole

Narration: None

Jim Quince is hot on the heels of a rustler when he is stopped by a group of ranchers and accused of the crime. Rowdy and Teddy prevent the ranchers from hanging Jim and Joe Scarlett, but their problems are not over.

Notes: Quince asks Favor to be taken off cutting and branding duty for a while as he's had "a belly full of rope."

#73: Incident Near Gloomy River
(March 17, 1961)

Director:	R.G. Springsteen
Writer:	John Dunkel
Cast:	John Cassavetes, John Ericson, Leif Erickson, Rosemary de Camp, Anne Helm

Narration: None

The drovers discover that a creek needed to water the herd has been dammed by feuding ranchers.

Notes: Leif Erickson later starred as John Cannon on *The High Chaparral*. His ranch house is the same used in several episodes as far back as "Incident at Jacob's Well" in 1959. Contrary to earlier episodes, Favor pays off a drover before the drive is done.

#74: Incident of the Boomerang
(March 24, 1961)

Director:	Allen Reisner
Story:	Michael Pate

Brinegar, Eastwood, Wooley and Fleming in "Incident of the Boomerang."
PHOTO COURTESY OF LANNY TUCKER.

TELEPLAY: Charles Larson
CAST: Patricia Medina, Woody Strode, Michael Pate, James Drury, Frank de Kova, John Cole, John Erwin, Charles Stevens

In Comanche country, the drive is joined by an Australian rancher, his shady fiancée, an outlaw on the run and a boomerang expert named Binnaburra.

NOTES: Unique episode. Individual shots of the cast accompany the opening credits. Australian actor Michael Pate, who contributed the story, speaks with his native accent. The drovers get their own boomerangs, and Wishbone's beloved stove is dropped in a mud puddle. James Drury later starred for nine seasons on NBC's *The Virginian*.

Woody Strode and extras on the set of "Incident of the Boomerang."

#75: Incident of His Brother's Keeper
(March 31, 1961)

Director:	Ted Post
Writer:	Buckley Angell
Cast:	Jack Lord, Susan Oliver, Jeff Richards, Norman Leavitt, Viola Harris, Alan Reynolds, Dick Winslow, Margie Liszt, Fenton G. Jones

Narration: "There's one good thing you can say about drivin' a herd up the Sedalia Trail. Beeves stay beeves. The drovers stay human, and trouble is always saddlin' up a fresh horse, preparin' to ride with you. What you can't be sure of is the direction it's comin' from, the face it's gonna be wearin', the name it'll be travelin' under. What you can be sure of is that trouble knows your name. Mine's Gil Favor, trail boss."

Pete and Wishbone ride into Miracle Springs to check cattle prices and locate a hot spring and mud bath for Wishbone's ailing back. Pete becomes involved with a crippled rancher and his long suffering young wife.

Notes: Jack Lord and Susan Oliver, who play the married couple, were also romantically linked characters in an episode of *Bonanza* the previous year.

#76: Incident in the Middle of Nowhere
(April 7, 1961)

Director:	R.G. Springsteen
Story:	Howard Rigsby & Louis Vittes
Teleplay:	Louis Vittes
Cast:	Cecil Kellaway, Fay Spain, Elisha Cook, George Keymas, James Griffith, Charles Fredericks, X Brands, Olan Soule, Ralph Smiley

Searching for water, Favor and Rowdy hear classical music and discover a company of ballerinas performing for an elderly prospector. The old man tells the drovers he knows a way to get the herd through the Dead Mountains—then disappears.

Notes: Cecil Kellaway received an Academy Award nomination for

1948's *The Luck of the Irish*. Fay Spain guest starred on more than twenty Western series, including three episodes of *Rawhide*, and was only 50 years old when she died in 1983.

#77: INCIDENT OF THE PHANTOM BUGLER
(APRIL 14, 1961)

DIRECTOR: George B. Templeton
STORY: Buckley Angell & Louis Vittes
TELEPLAY: Louis Vittes
NARRATION: (Nearly identical to Episode #75)
CAST: Jock Mahoney, Vaughn Taylor, Kathie Browne, Hardie Albright, Robert Cabal, Ken Mayer, Richard Wolf, Jr., John Cole, Bill Cutter, John Erwin

The leader of an army of jayhawkers wants to establish a town on one of the main routes to the west. To finance the project he will not allow the drive to water the herd unless Favor pays him five dollars a head.

NOTES: Fleming and former stunt man Mahoney engage in a prolonged fight scene. Kathie Browne, who was on *Rawhide* three times, portrayed Pernell Roberts' romantic interest in a four episode arc on *Bonanza*. She also co-starred on the 1967 series *Hondo* and was in numerous other Westerns. She died at age 63 in 2003.

#78: INCIDENT OF THE LOST IDOL
(APRIL 28, 1961)

DIRECTOR: Ted Post
WRITER: Albert Aley
CAST: Claude Akins, Doug Lambert, Jena Engstrom, Robert Cabal, Ken Curtis, K.L Smith, Ted De Corsia, Gene Benton, Jean Engstrom, David MacMahon
NARRATION: None

Pete and Rowdy stop the runaway wagon of a dying woman and her two children. The mother says her husband is dead, but he has recently escaped from prison and has bounty hunters on his trail.

NOTES: A larger part than usual for Robert Cabal. Actresses Jena and Jean Engstrom were mother and daughter. Ken Curtis portrayed Festus on *Gunsmoke* for eleven seasons.

#79: INCIDENT OF THE RUNNING MAN
(MAY 5, 1961)

DIRECTOR: Justus Addis
WRITER: David Lang
CAST: Lloyd Corrigan, Donald Barry, Robert Wilke, Luana Anders, Walter Coy, Pete Mamakos, Pete Adams, Russ Conway, James Anderson, Helen Wallace, Glenn Dixon, Lew Brown, Gregg Martell, Terry Frost, Les Hellman, Jack Searl, Robert Donner, Robert Adler, Reg Parton
NARRATION: None

A sheriff does not believe Rowdy's story about a gang of outlaws who plan to take over a nearby army post and terrorize the territory.

NOTES: An action-filled Rowdy episode all the way. This was the first acting job by Eastwood's friend Robert Donner, later Yancy Tucker for seven seasons of *The Waltons*. Western fans will recognize Donald Barry as Don "Red" Barry, star of scores of films for more than thirty years, beginning in 1939. He died in 1980. Equally as accomplished was Robert J. Wilke, whose career spanned over forty years and countless television Westerns, including three episodes of *Rawhide*.

#80: INCIDENT OF THE PAINTED LADY
(MAY 12, 1961)

DIRECTOR: Harmon Jones
WRITER: John Dunkel
CAST: David Brian, Marie Windsor, Ed Nelson, Raymond Guth, Herbert Peterson, Don Harvey,

Harry Lauter, Paul Barselou, Byron Morrow,
Ted Stanhope

NARRATION: "Sometimes it gets right peaceful on a trail drive. You're travelin' easy in pretty country, with a trail broke herd actin' gentle as lambs. Weather's fine, air's fresh, sun's warm. That's when I begin to worry. Somethin's bound to happen. And out of all the bad things that might be, it usually turns out to be the kind of trouble you least expect. My name's Gil Favor, trail boss."

An angry sheriff wants Favor to pay fifteen thousand dollars for a thousand cattle stolen by Thad Clemens, another trail boss. Because all Texans supposedly stick together. Favor finds Clemens in the Painted Lady Saloon and confronts him.

NOTES: Ed Nelson, who starred in the series *Peyton Place* and *The Silent Force*, was one of the busiest actors in the history of the medium. In addition to four episodes of *Rawhide*, he was a guest on nearly thirty other Westerns, including the first hour-long episode of *Gunsmoke*.

#81: INCIDENT BEFORE BLACK PASS
(MAY 19, 1961)

DIRECTOR: Ted Post
STORY: Arthur Rowe & Don Moore
TELEPLAY: Arthur Rowe, Don Moore & Louis Vittes
CAST: Zachary Scott, Robert Armstrong, Cathy Downs,
               Joan Taylor, Arthur Batanides, Dennis Cross,
               Leonard Nimoy, Robert Sampson, John Cole,
               Henry Gillen, Billy Strange, Reg Parton, Jimmy
               Lee Cook, Johnny Lomma

NARRATION: None

Pete and Rowdy are captured by renegade Kiowa warriors whose leader is a half-breed named White Eyes. The chief wants peace, but a local rancher is determined to kill him.

NOTES: Joan Taylor played storekeeper Milly Scott on *The Rifleman* for two seasons. Leonard Nimoy, best known as *Star Trek*'s Spock, also appeared in more than twenty different Western series.

#82: INCIDENT OF THE BLACKSTORMS
(MAY 26, 1961)

DIRECTOR: R.G. Springsteen
STORY: Sheb Wooley & Tony Habeeb
TELEPLAY: Jan Winters
CAST: Stephen McNally, Robert Crawford, Jr., Bern Hoffman, Virginia Christine, Val Avery, Harry Shannon, Richard Reeves, Tom Greenway, Milton Parsons, Dee Pollack, George Hickman

NARRATION: None

Outlaw Sky Blackstorm involves Pete and Mushy in his plan to kidnap his own son, who does not know his father is Blackstorm.

NOTES: An episode co-written by Sheb Wooley that features neither Fleming nor Eastwood. Robert Crawford, Jr., better known as Bobby, is the older brother of Johnny Crawford, *The Rifleman*'s Mark McCain. Bobby co-starred on *Laramie* for its first two seasons.

#83: INCIDENT OF THE NIGHT ON THE TOWN
(JUNE 2, 1961)

DIRECTOR: Tony Leader
STORY: Chris Miller & Eric Fleming
TELEPLAY: Louis Vittes
CAST: Harry Townes, James Drury, Margaret Hayes, Don Haggerty, Anne Whitfield, Ralph Dumke, Norman Leavitt, Grady Sutton, Elizabeth Furedi, Ralph Smiley, Allan Nixon, Tom Peters, Dorothy Christmas

Favor is served with a summons to appear in court in Bentley, Texas. The judge tells him he has several hundred cattle that do not belong to him.

NOTES: New opening showing drovers riding into town and in a saloon. Sheb Wooley and Paul Brinegar are depicted with Fleming and Eastwood in the credits for the first time. Also for the first time, Robert Cabal is credited in the closing titles even though he is not in the episode. Favor mentions his wife being dead.

Maggie Hayes, James Drury and Fleming in "Incident of the Night on the Town."

#84: Incident of the Wager on Payday
(June 16, 1961)

Director:	R.G. Springsteen
Writer:	Louis Vittes
Cast:	Stephen Joyce, Kathie Browne, Ford Rainey, Lurene Tuttle, Charles Watts, Mark Tapscott, Jonathan Hole, Percy Helton, Mickey Finn, Hank Patterson, Dick Ryan, David McMahon, Tom Wade, Larry Kent, Henry Wills, Ken Mayer

Rowdy is robbed of the drive's cashbox, but some of the drovers wonder if he took off with it. Favor bets Jim and Pete that Rowdy will return with the money by payday.

Notes: Different individual opening shots of Fleming, Eastwood, Wooley and Brinegar than in the previous episode. "Painted Lady" sign from episode #80 visible on street set. Robert Cabal again listed with regular cast in closing credits, but not in episode.

SEASON FOUR

#85: RIO SALADO
(SEPTEMBER 29, 1961)

WRITER: John Dunkel
DIRECTOR: Ted Post
CAST: Tom Tully, Edward Andrews, Carlos Romero, John
            Pickard, Alex Montoyo, Jan Arvan, Don Harvey,
            Penny Santon, John Erwin, Bert Remsen, Michael
            Davis, Tyler McVey, Kenneth MacDonald, Len
            Hendry

The Gil Favor outfit reunites for another drive in the same town where Rowdy's long lost father, Dan Yates, is living. Dan wants Rowdy to help him kill a Mexican bandit and split the reward.

NOTES: First season without producer Charles Marquis Warren. Endre Bohem reverses the director and writer credits and places them at the front of the episode. No more narration from Fleming or the other cast members. Favor tells the men this herd will be the first that is all his and he will share a quarter of his profits with the drovers.

#86: THE SENDOFF
(OCTOBER 2, 1961)

WRITER: John Dunkel
DIRECTOR: George B. Templeton
CAST: Darren McGavin, Claude Akins, Lillian
            Bronson, Stacy Harris, Don Harvey, John Hart,
            Charles Tannen, Edward Colmans, Kelly Dobson,

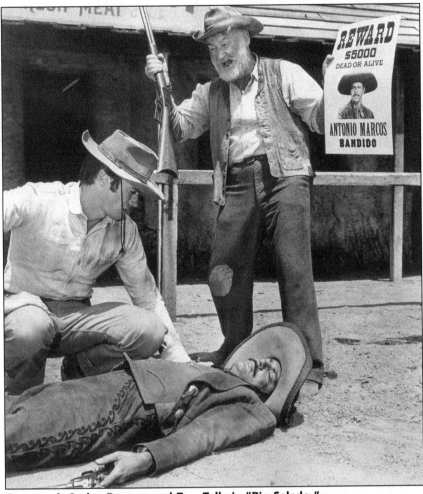

Eastwood, Carlos Romero and Tom Tully in "Rio Salado."

George Chalk, John Cole, William Thompkins,
Guy Teague

Beating the brush for scrub cattle, Favor discovers the ruins of a wagon train and a reclusive cowboy with cattle he says are not for sale.

NOTES: Episode shot entirely outdoors. Good performance by Darren McGavin, who was married to actress Kathie Browne. In a rare blooper, a truck can be seen in the distance during the final scene. The closing credits play over a continuation of the episode's last sequence.

#87: THE LONG SHAKEDOWN
(OCTOBER 13, 1961)

WRITER: Albert Aley
DIRECTOR: Justus Addiss
CAST: Skip Homeier, Lew Gallo, Don Harvey, Jay
             Douglas, Ed Faulkner, Kelly Dobson

Three days out of Laredo and headed for Abilene, Favor is discouraged with the drive's progress and the laziness of his men.

NOTES: Favor and Wishbone discuss the many years they have been driving cattle, noting that it gets a little harder each time. Favor says Quince, Scarlett and Collins are getting older, losing spirit, ability and agility.

#88: JUDGMENT AT HONDO SECO
(OCTOBER 20, 1961)

TELEPLAY: Louis Vittes
STORY: John Dunkel & Louis Vittes
DIRECTOR: Perry Lafferty
CAST: Ralph Bellamy, Burt Douglas, Anne Whitfield,
             Jean Inness, Roy Barcroft, Richard Wessel, Kathie
             Browne, Ray Teal, Tom Greenway, Robert Bice,
             George Petrie, Robert Donner, Henry Wills, Guy
             Cain

Jim Quince visits his brother Matt, a judge whom he has not seen in six years. Matt later accuses Jim of helping a prisoner escape and sentences him to be hanged.

NOTES: The drovers sing "No Place Like Home" around the campfire. Kathie Browne plays a character named Lily, the same name she had in "Incident of the Wager on Payday." Ray Teal portrayed Sheriff Roy Coffee for twelve of *Bonanza*'s fourteen seasons. Veteran actor Ralph Bellamy is credited as Special Guest Star at the top of the episode as well as in the end credits.

#89: THE LOST TRIBE
(OCTOBER 27, 1961)

WRITER: John Dunkel
DIRECTOR: George B. Templeton
CAST: Abraham Sofaer, Larry Chance, John Hart, John Erwin, Elizabeth Furedi, Bob Swimmer

At night on the Chisholm Trail, three Indians stampede the herd. Pete wants to go after the Indians by himself and will not say why.

NOTES: Pete reveals that he was once married. Distinctive character actor Abraham Sofaer appeared in more than fifteen television Westerns.

#90: THE INSIDE MAN
(NOVEMBER 3, 1961)

WRITER: Albert Aley
DIRECTOR: George B. Templeton
CAST: Charles Gray, Anne Helm, Chris Alcaide, Lane Bradford, Don Harvey

Trail boss Clay Forrester tells Favor he wants to quit the Roy Craddock outfit and join Favor's. What he does not say is that Craddick is plotting to steal Favor's herd.

NOTES: Charles Gray's first episode as Clay Forrester, a former army major, though not yet an official member of the drive. Opening features new shots of the cattle and Fleming, Eastwood, Brinegar and Wooley.

#91: THE BLACK SHEEP
(NOVEMBER 10, 1961)

TELEPLAY: Charles Larson
STORY: Jack Curtis
DIRECTOR: Tony Leader
CAST: Richard Basehart, Will Wright, Hardie Albright, Don Harvey, James Anderson, Clarke Gordon, Hal Baylor, Fred Graham

The drive butts heads with a shepherd and his flock. Rowdy says cattle will not eat or drink where sheep have been, and that his cousin was injured in a stampede caused by sheep.

Notes: When Jim Quince breaks his leg, Wishbone says, "It's broke good." Richard Basehart, who later starred in the series *Voyage to the Bottom of the Sea*, is credited both before and after the episode.

#92: The Prairie Elephant
(November 16, 1961)

Teleplay:	Louis Vittes
Story:	Walter Wagner & Louis Vittes
Director:	Robert L. Friend
Cast:	Lawrence Dobkin, Gloria Talbott, Britt Lomond, Billy Barty, Laurie Mitchell, Mickey Morton, Maxine Gates

The herd is spooked by the scent of lions coming from a line of circus wagons. To solve the problem, Favor offers to let Pete guide the wagons to Bradley, Texas, at no charge.

Notes: No Rowdy in this unusual episode. Elephants were novelties on several television Westerns (*Gunsmoke, Bonanza* and *Wanted Dead or Alive* among them). However, strangely, this episode's title creature has little to do with the story.

#93: The Little Fishes
(November 24, 1961)

Writer:	Charles Larson
Director:	Justus Addiss
Cast:	Burgess Meredith, Richard Webb, Phyllis Coates, Don Harvey, Richard Reeves, Russ Bender, Leake Bevil

Favor's rush to get the herd to Abilene before the market for beef crashes is impeded by a scientist who wants help getting a bowl of shad to the rivers of California.

NOTES: Burgess Meredith given credit both before and after the episode, a practice that becomes routine this season with big name guest stars. Endre Bohem's credit as producer precedes the names of the writer and director. The California Department of Fish and Game is thanked for their cooperation and information.

#94: THE BLUE SPY
(DECEMBER 8, 1961)

TELEPLAY:	Tom Seller
STORY:	Warren Douglas
DIRECTOR:	Sobey Martin
CAST:	Phyllis Thaxter, Lyle Bettger, Charles Aidman, George Wallace, Harry Lauter, John Cole, Reg Parton, Guy Cain

Pete sees some Indians wearing theatrical costumes stolen from a woman who staggers into camp. She claims to be an actress, but the drovers turn a cold shoulder to her when they learn she was a spy for the Union.

NOTES: William Thompkins, identified in later episodes as Toothless Jeffries, is among the drovers but receives no on-screen credit.

#95: THE GENTLEMAN'S GENTLEMAN
(DECEMBER 15, 1961)

WRITER:	J.E. Selby
DIRECTOR:	Sobey Martin
CAST:	Brian Aherne, John Sutton, Richard Shannon, Russell Thorson, Sheila Bromley, Kathryn Card, Don Harvey, Jay Silverheels, John Hart, Paul Barselow, Lane Chandler, Tim Graham, Mark Slade, Elizabeth Furedi

A British lord is killed while hunting buffalo, but before he dies he orders his valet to become Favor's servant, which does not go over well with the drovers.

Notes: No Rowdy in this episode. Jay Silverheels, who plays Pawnee Joe, will be forever known as the Lone Ranger's faithful companion Tonto.

#96: Twenty-Five Santa Clauses
(December 22, 1961)

WRITER: Charles Larson
DIRECTOR: Robert L. Friend
CAST: Ed Wynn, Anne Seymour, Rafael Lopez,
              Theodore Newton, Don Harvey, John Hart,
              Guy Cain

The drive takes in an elderly con man, his wife and a young boy, just in time for a swindle known as "The Christmas Game."

Notes: Charles Gray returns as Clay Forrester, though there is no explanation as to how he joined the drive. CBS no doubt wanted the episode to air just days before Christmas. (Sheb Wooley is in the opening credits, but Gray takes his place in the closing credits.) John Hart is billed as Narbo, a bespectacled drover, for the first time, though he is never referred to by name. Guy Cain plays drover McGann for the second time.

#97: The Long Count
(January 5, 1962)

WRITER: Albert Aley
DIRECTOR: Jesse Hibbs
CAST: Bethel Leslie, Charles Gray, Kevin Hagen, Harry
              Shannon, Robert Cornthwaite, Milton Frome,
              Cheerio Meredith, Charles Maxwell, Vito Scotti,
              Allegra Varron, Jack Boyle, John Day

Pete and Rowdy enter a barber shop and bump into Clay Forrester, now wearing a marshal's badge and working as a census taker instead of working as a drover. Rowdy later tells Clay to quit running around and rejoin Favor's outfit.

Notes: This episode (production #3014), which shows Clay officially joining the series, was filmed before "The Twenty-Five Santa Clauses" (#3022), but was broadcast two weeks later.

#98: THE CAPTAIN'S WIFE
(JANUARY 12, 1962)

WRITER: John Dunkel
DIRECTOR: Tay Garnett
CAST: Barbara Stanwyck, John Howard, Robert Lowery, Nestor Pavia, Eugene Martin, Dennis Cross, Bill Walker, Ross Ford, Mary Carroll, Johnny O'Neill, Val Benedict, Jerry Rush, John Hart

Favor and some of his men go to Fort Tracy for supplies and find it nearly deserted. The commanding officer's wife has deliberately made sure most of the soldiers go after warring Comancheros, leaving the fort undefended.

NOTES: A typically bravura performance by Barbara Stanwyck, who would later star in her own Western series, *The Big Valley*, for four seasons. No Rowdy or Pete in this episode. John Hart credited again as Narbo, though never called by name.

#99: THE PEDDLER
(JANUARY 19, 1962)

WRITER: Charles Larson
DIRECTOR: Laslo Benedek
CAST: Shelley Berman, Vitina Marcus, George Kennedy, William Tannen, Hal Jon Norman, Don Beddoe, I. Stanford Jolley, William Riggs, Elizabeth Furedi

Favor, Rowdy, Jim and Pete come upon a small herd belonging to Jewish peddler Mendel Sorkin, who wants only to return to his homeland. Sorkin tries to sell the herd to Favor, but the trail boss is badly in need of money, not more cows.

NOTES: Good stab at a dramatic performance by comedian Shelley Berman. George Kennedy, who would win an Oscar for 1967's *Cool Hand Luke*, appeared in more than twenty Western series early in his career. William Thompkins appears as Toothless, but still given no credit.

#100: The Woman Trap
(January 26, 1962)

Writer: Buckley Angell
Director: George B. Templeton
Cast: Robert Gist, Maria Palmer, Alan Hale, Karen Steele, Rayford Barnes, Carol Byron, Dorothy Dells, Ray Montgomery, Carole Kent, Gene Damion, Jim Galente, Marion Ross

The drovers come to the aid of a group of mail order brides whose escorts plan to hand them off to a gang of outlaws instead of their intended spouses.

Notes: Karen Steele made numerous Westerns on both the small and large screens. Marion Ross is best known as Marion Cunningham on the 1970s series *Happy Days*.

#101: The Boss's Daughters
(February 2, 1962)

Writer: Albert Aley
Director: Sobey Martin
Cast: Paul Richards, Dorothy Green, Cindy Moore, Barbara Beaird, Byron Morrow, Harry Fleer, Vici Raaf, Joe Brooks, Red Morgan

The drive is prevented from crossing the land of Vance Caldwell, a rancher who has invited Favor's daughters and sister-in-law to visit his place.

Notes: A sequel of sorts to "Incident of the Fish Out of Water." Second and final appearance of Favor's girls, who get to deliver the order to "Head 'em up, move 'em out!" No Rowdy. Toothless in episode but not identified.

Carole Kent, Fleming, Karen Steele, and others in "The Woman Trap."

#102: The Deserter's Patrol
(February 9, 1962)

WRITER: Louis Vittes

DIRECTOR: Andrew V. McLaglen

CAST: Jock Gaynor, Don Megowan, Robert Dix, Russell Arms, Russ Conway, Dan Stafford, Conlan Carter, Ed Faulkner, Will J. White, Hal Needham, Barnaby Hale, Bob Duggan, Harry Carey, Jr.

Six soldiers desert from Fort Brace and are captured by warring Pawnees led by Ogalla, the chief that Pete, Favor and Wishbone rescued while in Philadelphia.

NOTES: Another follow-up episode to "Incident of the Fish Out of Water." No Rowdy or Wishbone. Sheb Wooley's last show as a cast regular.

#103: THE GREEDY TOWN
(FEBRUARY 16, 1962)

TELEPLAY:	Tom Seller
STORY:	Lew Lantz
DIRECTOR:	Murray Golden
CAST:	Mercedes McCambridge, Jim Davis, Diana Millay, J. Pat O'Malley, Kathleen Freeman, Ross Elliott, William Phipps, Dean Fredericks, Addison Richards, Roy E. Glenn, Sr., Fred Lerner, Chuck Hicks, Jim Galante

A woman in Dry Rock offers Clay Forrester two thousand dollars to give testimony that will clear her dead son's name and run a crooked sheriff out of town.

NOTES: Fourth episode with Charles Gray as Clay Forrester, but in opening credits for the first time. No Gil Favor. Western veteran Jim Davis starred in *Stories of the Century*, which earned an Emmy Award in 1954. He later portrayed Jock Ewing on the series *Dallas*.

#104: GRANDMA'S MONEY
FEBRUARY 23, 1962)

TELEPLAY:	J.E. Selby
STORY:	Sonia Chernus
DIRECTOR:	Sobey Martin
CAST:	Josephine Hutchinson, Frank Maxwell, Jonathan Hole, Frank Wilcox, Harry Ellerbe, Carol Ann Daniels, James Gavin, Thomas B.

Henry, Olan Soule, Everett Glass, Daniel M.
White, Norman Leavitt, Gayla Graves,
Roy Wright, Mason Curry, Claudia Perkins,
Zon Murray

Rowdy, Wishbone and Clay have three hundred head of cattle for a rancher whom they discover has gone off on his honeymoon. Rowdy then runs into an elderly woman bogged down in a buggy stolen from the rancher.

NOTES: Second episode in a row without Favor. Story contributed by Clint Eastwood's longtime friend Sonia Chernus. Josephine Hutchinson is best known to horror film fans as the doctor's wife in 1939's *Son of Frankenstein*.

#105: THE PITCHWAGON
(MARCH 2, 1962)

TELEPLAY: Lou Morheim & Wilton Schiller
STORY: Wilton Schiller
DIRECTOR: Sobey Martin
CAST: Buddy Ebsen, Hugh Marlowe, Joan O'Brien,
              Jack Elam, Nick Pawl, Dan Grayam, Ed Foster,
              Clancy Cooper, Russell Trent, Ralph Reed, John
              Hart, George Hickman, Larry Kent, Bud Osborne,
              Gail Bonney, Joe Brooks

Rowdy, Clay and a young drover save George Stimson, proprietor of a traveling medicine show, from Indians. The drover is killed, and Stimson suggests they get in a crooked poker game in a nearby town to raise money for the drover's widow and children.

NOTES: Still no sign of Favor, but most of the other drovers given more screen time than usual. Eastwood sings the Russ Garcia/Lenny Adelson number "Beyond the Sun," the secondary theme of the series, and gives the order to "Head 'em up, move 'em out!" Although Jack Elam guest starred on nearly fifty Western series, this was his only appearance on *Rawhide*. In 1983 he was given one of the very first Golden Boot Awards. He died in 2003 at the age of 82.

#106: THE HOSTAGE CHILD
(MARCH 9, 1962)

WRITER: Bronson Howitzer
DIRECTOR: Harmon Jones
CAST: Debra Paget, James Coburn, Edward Kemmer,
                Jimmy Baird, Naomi Stevens, Alan Reynolds,
                Joe Brooks

A young Indian boy tells the drovers he is on his way to join his sister at Fort Lacy. Clay tells Rowdy and Favor that the fort is run by Colonel Briscoe, a well known Indian hater.

NOTES: Academy Award winner James Coburn toiled long and hard on the video range, guest starring on more than thirty series. This was his only *Rawhide*.

#107: THE IMMIGRANTS
MARCH 16, 1962)

WRITER: Elliott Arnold
DIRECTOR: Tay Garnett
CAST: John Van Dreelan, Maria Palmer, Robert Boon,
                John Mauldin, Jim Galante, Don Hight

Clay, Jim and Wishbone may have come into contact with anthrax, so they isolate themselves from the rest of the drovers, only to be taken prisoner by a German count who says they are trespassing on his land.

NOTES: Jim makes a reference to the Swiss settlers encountered in "Incident of the Music Maker." Same stone ranch house used in numerous episodes from "Incident at Jacob's Well" on. Favor once again missing in action.

#108: THE CHILD-WOMAN
(MARCH 23, 1962)

TELEPLAY: Elliott Arnold
STORY: Carey Wilbur
DIRECTOR: Murray Golden

CAST: Cesar Romero, Jena Engstrom, Dorothy Morris, Julian Burton, John Hart, Coke Willis, George Barrows, Dick Winslow

The drive reaches the town of Buffalo Wells, where Mushy has two cousins, one of them an actress who performs at the Longhorn Saloon. She begs Mushy to get her younger sister out of town and away from town boss Big Tim Sloan.

NOTES: No sign of Rowdy. William Thompkins appears as one of Big Tim's henchman rather than Toothless Jeffries.

#109: A WOMAN'S PLACE
(MARCH 30, 1962)

WRITERS: Eric Fleming & Chris Miller
DIRECTOR: Justus Addiss
CAST: Gail Kobe, Jacques Aubuchon, Eduard Franz, Mala Powers, Charles Maxwell, Herbert Patterson, Robert B. Williams, Marilee Phelps, John Close, John Alvin, Alex Barringer, Reg Parton, Mark Tanny

When the chuck wagon breaks down and crushes a drover's ribs, the only doctors available are a quack and a woman the townspeople do not consider capable.

NOTES: Second script written by Eric Fleming and Chris Miller. Charles Maxwell, usually cast as a villain in dozens of Westerns, plays a sheriff for a change. Technical advisor for this episode was Dr. Michael Saleh, named in closing credits.

#110: REUNION
(APRIL 6, 1962)

WRITER: Elliott Arnold
DIRECTOR: Sobey Martin
CAST: Walter Pidgeon, Darryl Hickman, Judson Pratt, Eugene Iglesias, William Wellman, Jr., John Hart, Guy Cain, Anthony Caruso

Brinegar, Gail Kobe and Fleming in "A Woman's Place."

With water becoming scarce, Wishbone finds a flag of Texas planted in the middle of nowhere, and an arrow made of rocks pointing to water. And there is also a note from Pete Nolan, who is no longer with the drive.

NOTES: Sheb Wooley is billed with the guest cast as "Also Starring." Not a complete reunion as Rowdy is not in the episode. William Wellman, Jr., is billed as Sergeant Bennett, although he is referred to as Corporal Bennett. Walter Pidgeon was a distinguished screen actor whose credits date as far back as 1925. In 1940 he co-starred in *Dark Command,* the only film to team Roy Rogers and John Wayne.

Wooley and Walter Pidgeon in "Reunion."

#111: House of the Hunter
(April 20, 1962)

WRITER: Louis Vittes
DIRECTOR: Tay Garnett
CAST: Robert F. Simon, Rosemary De Camp, Paula
Raymond, Lester Matthews, Peter Adams, Lane
Bradford, Harry Shannon, Hal Jon Norman

Hey-Soos predicts that someone is bringing death to the drive the night before Rowdy stumbles into a strange house where a group of people have been imprisoned by unknown captors.

NOTES: Familiar "Jacob's Well" ranch house once again.

#112: Gold Fever
(May 4, 1962)

TELEPLAY: J.E. Selby
STORY: Sid Harris
DIRECTOR: James P. Yarbrough
CAST: Victor Jory, Karen Sharpe, Adam Williams, Marion
Ross, Davey Davison, Logan Field, Charles
Tannen, Quentin Sondergaard, Glen Gordon, Ted
Stanhope, Curt Barrett, Ron Brogan

When an old prospector gives Wishbone gold dust in exchange for a shovel and pick, the drovers figure there is a fortune waiting in the ghost town up ahead. Favor warns them that Rowdy will hire men to replace them if they quit to look for gold.

NOTES: Karen Sharpe played Laura Thomas on the series *Johnny Ringo*.

#113: The Devil and the Deep Blue
(May 11, 1962)

TELEPLAY: Louis Vittes
STORY: Endre Bohem
DIRECTOR: George B. Templeton
CAST: Coleen Gray, Tod Andrews, Ted de Corsia,

John Pickard, Harry Lauter, Len Hendry, John Erwin, John Hart, George Hickman, Larry Kent, Guy Cain, Bob Swimmer

Favors stops the drive short of Abilene to let the cattle fatten up first, not knowing the herd coming up from behind contains cows sick with Texas tic fever.

NOTES: Favor reminds Rowdy that all the drovers have a stake in the herd on this drive. One of the best episodes of the season, written by producer Endre Bohem.

#114: ABILENE
(MAY 18, 1962)

TELEPLAY: Charles Larson & Elliott Arnold
STORY: Charles Larson
DIRECTOR: Tony Leader
CAST: Audrey Totter, Ken Lynch, John Pickard, Bing Russell, John Collier, E.J. Andre, Stacy Graham, James Secrest, John Erwin, William Thompkins, John Hart, Dick Winslow, Joe Brooks, Kent Hays, John Cole, Guy Teague

The sheriff in Abilene orders the drovers quarantined in the hotel for at least four days when the doctor says one of them may have smallpox. This is bad news for Favor, who has to get to Missouri before his option on some land expires.

NOTES: Favor says he is considering giving up being a trail boss and settling down with his daughters. Oddly, neither Mushy nor Hey-Soos appear in the episode, though William Thompkins is called Toothless and given billing for the first time. Bing Russell played Deputy Clem Foster on *Bonanza* for eleven seasons. Final episode filmed at MGM.

SEASON FIVE

#115: INCIDENT OF THE HUNTER
(SEPTEMBER 28, 1962)

TELEPLAY: Charles Larson
STORY: D.D. Beauchamp
DIRECTOR: Thomas Carr
CAST: Mark Stevens, Gregory Walcott, Hal Baylor,
                William Thompkins

On the trail to Denver, Rowdy recognizes a man who rides into camp as Colonel John Shephard, a fellow prisoner of war back in 1861. When Clay says Shephard is actually a bounty hunter from the Dakotas named Rankin, the drovers turn on the man.

NOTES: Production now at CBS Studio City. New opening depicting a map of trail drive routes. New credit listings—without pictures—for Fleming, Eastwood, Brinegar and Gray. Back to referring to stories as incidents, as initiated by original producer Charles Marquis Warren for seasons one through three. Episode title shown in the middle of screen instead of lower right corner. Credit for new producer Vincent M. Fennelly given in closing titles rather than up front.

#116: INCIDENT OF THE PORTRAIT
(OCTOBER 5, 1962)

WRITERS: William Blinn & Michael Gleason
DIRECTOR: Ted Post
CAST: John Ireland, Nina Shipman, Ted de Corsia,
                Emile Meyer

Outlaw Frank Trask accidentally kills the father of a blind young woman and finds refuge with the Gil Favor outfit. Later, a sheriff asks if the drive will escort the woman to the next town—and Favor assigns Trask to drive her wagon.

NOTES: One of the best episodes of the series, with an outstanding job by John Ireland. Although Charles Gray does not appear, there is an effort to give the whole cast something to say or do, a trend that will continue throughout the season.

#117: INCIDENT AT CACTUS WELLS
(OCTOBER 12, 1962)

WRITER: Albert Aley
DIRECTOR: Christian Nyby
CAST: Keenan Wynn, Ron Hagerthy, Henry Wills,
              Don Haggerty

Favor hires Simon Royce, who has been shadowing the herd, then learns the man is wanted for murdering his wife. Royce swears he has been acquitted of the crime.

NOTES: Episode title not in Western style lettering. When Clay says it might not be a good idea to hire Royce, Favor reminds him that he once tried to move in from the inside and take over the herd ("The Inside Man").

#118: INCIDENT OF THE PRODIGAL SON
(OCTOBER 19, 1962)

WRITER: Richard Fielder
DIRECTOR: Christian Nyby
CAST: Gene Evans, Carl Reindel, Frank Wilcox

Sam Hargis, one of Favor's older drovers, takes a liking to a rude young man who reminds him of his dead son. When Hargis is fired from the drive, the young man asks if he can join him in starting up a horse ranch.

NOTES: A particularly good episode with an outstanding performance by Gene Evans. No sign of Mushy, though he is mentioned. Carl Reindel guest starred on several television Westerns and played the same character in two episodes of *Gunsmoke*. He died in 2009 at the age of seventy-four.

#119: Incident of the Four Horsemen
(October 26, 1962)

WRITER: Charles Larson
DIRECTOR: Thomas Carr
CAST: John Dehner, Claude Akins, Ron Hayes, Jena Engstrom, Robert Wilke, James Griffith, Roberto Contreras, Myron Healey, Edward Faulkner, I. Stanford Jolley, Norman Leavitt

The drive rides into the middle of a range war. The drovers bury a supposedly dead man, but while Wishbone pounds the grave marker down, a hand rises out of the earth.

NOTES: A somewhat muddled story despite a sterling cast. No Rowdy. Ron Hayes and Myron Healey each made countless television Westerns.

#120: Incident of the Lost Woman
(November 2, 1962)

WRITER: Ward Hawkins
DIRECTOR: Thomas Carr
CAST: Fay Spain, R.G. Armstrong, Dean Stanton, Hampton Fancher, Roy Engel

Favor finds an unconscious woman and her infant stranded on the prairie and takes them back to camp. Later, three hill men from Tennessee ride in and order the woman to come with them.

NOTES: Dean Stanton, now known as Harry Dean Stanton, appeared in more than twenty Western series, including three episodes of *Rawhide*. Hampton Fancher guest starred on more than fifteen Westerns and appeared on *Rawhide* twice.

#121: INCIDENT OF THE DOGFACES
(NOVEMBER 9, 1962)

WRITER: Gene L. Coon
DIRECTOR: Don McDougall
CAST: James Whitmore, John Doucette, Steve Brodie, James Beck, Robert J. Stevenson, William Wellman, Jr., Ford Rainey

Rowdy, Jim and Clay come to the rescue of three army troopers pinned down by Comanches. Sergeant Duclos says they are scouting land for settlers even though a treaty has given the territory to Chief Broken Bow.

NOTES: Another highpoint of the series. James Whitmore guest starred on more than fifteen television Westerns, twice playing a soldier on *Rawhide.*

#122: INCIDENT OF THE WOLVERS
(NOVEMBER 16, 1962)

WRITER: William L. Stuart
DIRECTOR: Thomas Carr
CAST: Dan Duryea, Patty McCormack, Paul Carr, Jack Grinnage

In country with a shortage of small game, the drovers know the herd is in danger from wolves. A man named Cannon says he and his crew will fight off the predators in exchange for fifty head of beef.

NOTES: Although Favor is supposed to off selling beef to the army, he delivers the "Head 'em up, move 'em out!" command at the end of the episode. When his big screen career faded, Dan Duryea found a second home on the video range, guest starring on more than fifteen different series, including three episodes of *Rawhide.*

#123: INCIDENT AT SUGAR CREEK
(NOVEMBER 23, 1962)

WRITER: Fred Freiberger
DIRECTOR: Christian Nyby

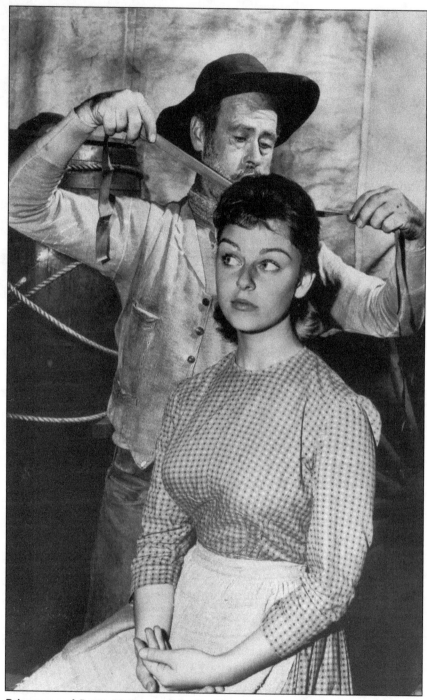

Brinegar and Patty McCormack in "Incident of the Wolvers."

CAST: Everett Sloane, Beverly Garland, John Larch,
Arthur Franz, James Westerfield, John Litel,
Charles Herbert, Jack Kosslyn

Drover Sam Garrett, a former convict, is trampled by the cattle outside the town of Sugar Creek. The local doctor will not return to the drive with Rowdy when he hears the injured man is Garrett.

NOTES: Brief glimpse of William Thompkins as Toothless. John Larch co-starred in Clint Eastwood's first directorial effort *Play Misty for Me* (1971).

#124: INCIDENT OF THE RELUCTANT BRIDEGROOM
(NOVEMBER 30, 1962)

TELEPLAY: Winston Miller
STORY: Tom Seller & William Driskill
DIRECTOR: Don McDougall
CAST: Ruta Lee, Arch Johnson, Ed Nelson, Harry Lauter,
Jack Kosslyn, Rodney Bell, Edward Foster, Curt
Barrett, Jack Boyle

Hotel owner John Landy refuses to marry Shelia Delancey but says he will kill any man that comes near her. Under the influence of a knockout drug the bartender slips into their drinks, Rowdy and Sheila are married by an outlaw posing as a preacher.

NOTES: Rare humorous episode. Ruta Lee was one of the busiest women on television, appearing in more than twenty Western series. This was the first of her two guest roles on *Rawhide*.

#125: INCIDENT OF THE QUERENCIAS
(DECEMBER 7, 1962)

WRITER: Joseph Petracca
DIRECTOR: Thomas Carr
CAST: Edward Andrews, Hal Baylor

The man who gave Favor his first job as trail boss has fallen on hard times and wants to drive join the drive with the thirty cattle he has left. Hey-Soos says the cows are called querencias—pasture

Brinegar and Ruta Lee in "Incident of the Reluctant Bridegroom."

cattle—that do not like to travel and get more difficult to handle the farther they get from home.

NOTES: Hal Baylor is listed as drover Jenkins with the rest of the regular cast, but William Thompkins (Toothless) again receives no credit.

#126: INCIDENT AT QUIVIRA
(DECEMBER 14, 1962)

WRITER: Ralphael Hayes
DIRECTOR: Christian Nyby
CAST: Royal Dano, Claude Akins, Donald Losby, William
             Henry, John Dierkes, Robert Kline

An old man stumbles into camp ranting that he has found Coronado's legendary city of gold in New Mexico's Guadalupe Mountains. He says he will share the gold with the drovers, and also show them the location of a fountain of youth. Only Mushy believes him.

NOTES: The prospector says he and Mushy feel the same as they have "simple souls" and that they will have to fight their way into Paradise because "them that's got it don't want to share." The first of Royal Dano's four *Rawhide* appearances. Dano was in constant demand during the heyday of the television Western, guest starring on nearly forty different series.

#127: INCIDENT OF DECISION
(DECEMBER 28, 1962)

WRITER: John Dunkel
DIRECTOR: Don McDougall
CAST: Doug Lambert, Carlos Romero, Hugh Sanders,
             Sheila Bromley, Michael de Anda

Rowdy will not allow a crippled boy who wants to be a drover to join the drive, but the boy follows anyway—and is taken hostage by Mexican bandits.

NOTES: Rowdy again gives the command to "Head 'em up, move 'em out!" A shot of Rowdy, Jim and Hey-Soos herding cattle plays under the closing credits rather than the generic shot of cattle going up a wooded slope used during this season. Carlos Romero, who died in 2007 at age eighty, made five episodes of *Rawhide*.

#128: INCIDENT OF THE BURYIN' MAN
(JANUARY 4, 1963)

WRITER: Jack Turley
DIRECTOR: Thomas Carr
CAST: King Donovan, Constance Ford, Richard Devon

A man driving a wagon with Funeral Service painted on it joins the drive and seems to have an endless supply of money when playing cards with the drovers.

NOTES: Jim calls Toothless by name, though William Thompkins still not included in the credits. Richard Devon, who guest starred on more than forty television Westerns, appeared on *Rawhide* this one time. He died in 2010 at the age of eighty-four.

#129: INCIDENT OF THE TRAIL'S END
(JANUARY 11, 1963)

WRITER: Ed Adamson
DIRECTOR: Don MacDougall
CAST: Harold J. Stone, George Brenlin, King Calder,
              Glenn Strange, Dwayne Spratt

Favor invites his mentor to join the drive, unaware that the older man has been diagnosed with glaucoma and is slowly going blind.

NOTES: Rowdy once again sings "Beyond the Sun." Favor hears and shakes his head, as though painful to hear. Glenn Strange, who was portraying bartender Sam on *Gunsmoke* at this time, appears as the bartender in the saloon where Rowdy performs.

#130: INCIDENT AT SPIDER ROCK
(JANUARY 18, 1963)

WRITER: Al C. Ward
DIRECTOR: Thomas Carr
CAST: Susan Oliver, Lon Chaney, James Best, William
              Phipps, Mary Beth Hughes

The drive stops for supplies, but what they buy is switched for inferior goods while they are finding watered down whiskey, rigged gambling tables and marked cards at the saloon.

NOTES: James Best, who appeared in three episodes of *Rawhide*, was a guest on more than forty Western series. He portrayed Sheriff Roscoe P. Coltrane on the long running series *The Dukes of Hazzard.*

#131: INCIDENT OF THE MOUNTAIN MAN
(JANUARY 25, 1963)

WRITER: Richard Fielder
DIRECTOR: Don McDougall
CAST: Robert Middleton, Patricia Crowley, Robert Wilke, Roy Barcroft, Hal Jon Norman

A woman pleads with Rowdy and Toothless to help her father, a wagon train scout accused of killing the wagonmaster's son.

NOTES: Story begins with a teaser before the episode title and writing and directing credits. Robert Middleton, Patricia Crowley and Roy Barcroft were all seasoned character actors with extensive Western credits, particularly Barcroft, veteran of scores of B-Westerns dating back as far as 1938.

#132: INCIDENT AT CROOKED HAT
(FEBRUARY 1, 1963)

WRITER: Joseph Petracca
DIRECTOR: Don McDougall
CAST: James Gregory, Jeanne Cooper, Arch Johnson, Parley Baer, Walter Sande, Jan Merlin, Robert J. Stevenson, Harlan Warde

Owen Spencer, a reformed gunman working for Favor, is challenged by a hot headed young drover who knows of Spencer's reputation.

NOTES: Pretty basic story elevated by good writing and Gregory's effective performance. The versatile actor guest starred on more than twenty Westerns, including three episodes of *Rawhide*, and was memorable as Inspector Frank Luger on the sitcom *Barney Miller.*

Eastwood and Claude Rains in "Incident of Judgment Day."

#133: INCIDENT OF JUDGMENT DAY
(FEBRUARY 3, 1963)

TELEPLAY: Paul King & Richard Landau
STORY: Richard Landau
DIRECTOR: Thomas Carr
CAST: Claude Rains, John Dehner, John Kellogg, Richard
              Carlyle, Howard Dayton, Gail Kobe

Rowdy's birthday celebration is interrupted when two men show up and say they have a score to settle. He rides with them to a ghost town where he is put on trial for committing an act of treason while a Union prisoner in 1864.

NOTES: The year is said to be 1871. The drovers sing "For He's a Jolly Good Fellow" during the celebration: this popular song dates back to 1709. The only other television Western done by distinguished actor Claude Rains was *Wagon Train*.

#134: INCIDENT OF THE GALLOWS TREE
(FEBRUARY 22, 1963)

TELEPLAY: Albert Aley
STORY: William L. Stuart
DIRECTOR: Christian Nyby
CAST: Beverly Garland, Gregory Walcott, Edward Faulkner, William Henry, Mike Ragan, Judson Pratt

Waking after a night of drinking in Cottonwood, Jim Quince discovers that the other drovers have gone back to their camp. He rides leisurely out of town, not knowing he is about to be arrested for murdering the mayor.

NOTES: A larger than usual part for Steve Raines. Beverly Garland appeared in more than twenty Western series, including three episodes of *Rawhide*. In 1986 she became one of the few women to win a Golden Boot Award. She died in 2008 at the age of 82.

#135: INCIDENT OF THE MARRIED WIDOW
(MARCH 1, 1963)

TELEPLAY: Paul King
STORY: Charles Gray & Kathleen Freeman
DIRECTOR: Thomas Carr
CAST: Patricia Barry, Dabbs Greer, Don Haggerty, Sheila Bromley, Roy Engel, Robert B. Williams

Rowdy spots a photograph of Favor in his Confederate uniform behind the bar of the Silver Slipper Saloon, along with a plaque saying the trail boss is dead. Even more disturbing is the pretty saloon owner's claim that Favor was her husband.

NOTES: Co-writer Charles Gray intended this episode to be about his character, Clay Forrester, but producer Vincent Fennelly had story editor Paul King rewrite it for Gil Favor. Rowdy sings for the third time in the series.

#136: Incident of the Pale Rider
(March 15, 1963)

Writer: Dean Riesner
Director: Christian Nyby
Cast: Albert Salmi, Fredd Wayne, Russell Thorson, Jack Searl, I. Stanford Jolley, Chubby Johnson

Rowdy kills a drunk attempting to steal two hundred dollars of the drive's money. A few days later, a drover identical to the dead man shows up in camp.

Notes: When Hey-Soos says a town has "the feel of death" Rowdy tells him to be superstitious on his own time. Albert Salmi guest starred on more than twenty-five Western series. He also co-starred on the first season of *Daniel Boone*, which would be produced by current *Rawhide* producer Vincent Fennelly. Character actor Chubby Johnson appeared in countless big and small screen Westerns.

#137: Incident of the Comanchero
(March 22, 1963)

Writer: Al C. Ward
Director: Thomas Carr
Cast: Robert Loggia, Virginia Gregg, Christopher Dark, Than Wyenn, Joseph Perry, Nina Shipman

After finding an ancient Indian torture rack, the drovers hear shots and discover two nuns caring for an injured man Jim assumes is an Indian.

Notes: No Favor in this talky episode that is more of a character study than a typical *Rawhide*. Favor, however, issues the familiar command at the end. No credit for Toothless even though he is given some lines of dialogue.

Eddie Bracken and Brinegar in "Incident of the Clown."

#138: INCIDENT OF THE CLOWN
(MARCH 29, 1963)

WRITER: Charles Larson
DIRECTOR: Don McDougall
CAST: Eddie Bracken, Harry Lauter, Ted de Corsia, Richard Hale, Joey Russo

Well-meaning but naïve Morris G. Stevens believes that his compiling a Comanche/English dictionary will prevent war between the two races. In the meantime, he tells the drovers he needs a doctor for the son of Chief Lame Bear. If his son dies, Lame Bear has vowed to kill all white men.

NOTES: Brief, final appearance by Charles Gray as Clay Forrester. Comic actor Eddie Bracken's two episodes of *Rawhide* were his only television Western credits.

#139: INCIDENT OF THE BLACK ACE
(APRIL 12, 1963)

WRITER: Dean Riesner
DIRECTOR: Thomas Carr
CAST: Walter Slezak, Robert Strauss, Chris Alcaide, Karen Sharpe

Wishbone tells Favor he is tired of being teased about his cooking and taken for granted. A fortune teller says Wishbone will die unless he leaves the drive.

NOTES: The gypsy tells Rowdy he will eventually meet a dark haired woman and have five children. Movie actor Walter Slezak made only one other television Western, an episode of *The Outlaws*.

#140: INCIDENT OF THE HOSTAGES
(APRIL 19, 1963)

TELEPLAY: Charles Larson
STORY: Paul King
DIRECTOR: Don McDougall
CAST: Leslie Wales, Suzanne Cupito, Rodolfo Acosta, William R. Thompkins, Joseph Perry, Naomi Stevens, Tony Haig

An Arapaho Indian tells Rowdy, Jim and Joe that he will trade three white hostages rescued from the Apaches for forty head of cattle. However, the hostages, including two young children, want to return to the Apaches.

NOTES: One of the best episodes of the fifth season. Because of his daughters, Favor says he has a way with little girls. Actress Suzanne Cupito later changed her name to Morgan Brittany and co-starred on the TV series *Dallas*.

#141: INCIDENT OF THE WHITE EYES
(MAY 3, 1963)

TELEPLAY: Edward J. Lakso & Shimon Wincelberg
STORY: Paul King
DIRECTOR: Christian Nyby
CAST: Nehemiah Persoff, John Vivyan, Diana Millay,
              William Schallert, Nita Talbot

Apaches trap Favor and a group of stagecoach passengers in an isolated relay station, but the Indians are after only one of them.

NOTES: Familiar Western plot improved by sharp writing and acting. Co-writer Shimon Wincelberg contributed extensively to *Have Gun-Will Travel*.

#142: INCIDENT AT RIO DOLOROSO
(MAY 10, 1963)

WRITER: Paul King
DIRECTOR: Thomas Carr
CAST: Cesar Romero, Madlyn Rhue, Michael Ansara,
              Ernest Sarracino, Carlos Romero, William
              Thompkins, Martin Garralaga

Stopping in the New Mexico town of Rio Doloroso, Rowdy and Wishbone are told that the herd is trespassing and will have to turn back unless the drovers pay three dollars a head for every third cow.

NOTES: Michael Ansara starred as an Indian marshal in *Law of the Plainsman*, one of the more unique television Westerns and a spin-off of *The Rifleman*.

#143: Incident at Alkali Sink
(May 24, 1963)

Writer: Thomas Thompson
Director: Don McDougall
Cast: Russell Johnson, Ruta Lee, Roy Barcroft,
              I. Stanford Jolley, William Thompkins,
              Judson Pratt

The drive must contend with the threat of warring Cheyenne Indians, the usual lack of water, and a father who objects to his daughter marrying one of the drovers.

Notes: Jim, promoted to scout now that Clay is gone, tells Rowdy he almost got married once. Favor is said to be in Denver, but gives the command to get the drive moving. Russell Johnson, who made numerous television Westerns and portrayed Marshal Gib Scott on the *Black Saddle* series, is best remembered as The Professor on *Gilligan's Island*.

SEASON SIX

Neville Brand and Eastwood in "Incident of the Red Wind."

#144: INCIDENT OF THE RED WIND
(SEPTEMBER 26, 1963)

WRITER: Dean Reisner
DIRECTOR: Thomas Carr
CAST: Neville Brand

Crossing the desert, the drive encounters a mustanger who tells Favor he knows the best way to get the herd to badly needed water.

NOTES: New opening showing the drive in the desert, the previous season's trail map replaced by silhouettes of Fleming, Eastwood and Brinegar. James Murdock now listed with Fleming, Eastwood and Brinegar in the closing credits. William Thompkins included with Raines, Shahan and Cabal. Lone guest star Neville Brand later played Texas Ranger Reese Bennett for two seasons on NBC's *Laredo*.

#145: INCIDENT OF IRON BULL
(OCTOBER 3, 1963)

WRITER: Carey Wilbur
DIRECTOR: Christian Nyby
CAST: James Whitmore, Michael Ansara, R.X. Slattery,
            Judson Pratt, Ralph Moody

Some of the drovers object when Rowdy, in Favor's absence, hires a Comanche named Joseph to help with the drive. Favor returns with Colonel John Macklin, who knows Joseph and also hates Indians.

NOTES: Strong episode with solid performances by Whitmore, Ansara and Slattery. Slattery portrayed Sgt. McKenna on the Warner Bros. World War II series *The Gallant Men* the previous season.

#146: INCIDENT AT EL CRUCERO
(OCTOBER 10, 1963)

WRITER: Charles Larson
DIRECTOR: Earl Bellamy
CAST: Elizabeth Montgomery, Gene Evans, Parley Baer,
            Buddy Baer, Mike Ragan, John Craig, Richard
            Simmons, L.Q. Jones, Joi Lansing

The herd has gone without water for three days, but a woman rancher and her small army of ten brothers will not allow the drive to cross their land.

NOTES: Rare romantic interlude for Favor. *Gunsmoke* fans will recognize the saloon in El Crucero as the Long Branch set. Elizabeth Montgomery is best known as Samantha on the long running sitcom *Bewitched*. At this time L.Q. Jones was a semi-regular cast

Eastwood, Fleming, Richard X. Slattery and Rocky Shahan (left to right, foreground) in "Incident of Iron Bull."

member of *The Virginian*, portraying ranch hand Belden.

#147: INCIDENT OF THE TRAVELLIN' MAN
(OCTOBER 17, 1963)

WRITER: Paul King
DIRECTOR: Ted Post
CAST: Simon Oakland, Robert Middleton, Robert
             Donner, James Sikking

The drovers find an unconscious man wearing leg irons. He says he is a Tennessee sharecropper and was attempting to commit suicide, but three riders claim he pistol whipped an old rancher and shot a sheriff in the back.

NOTES: The fight scene between Eric Fleming and Simon Oakland is one of the most exciting of the series. The end of the episode is intriguingly ambiguous. Oakland made guest appearances on more than twenty television Westerns. James Sikking went on to portray Lt. Howard Hunter on the police drama *Hill Street Blues*.

#148: INCIDENT AT PARADISE
(OCTOBER 24, 1963)

WRITER: Charles Larson
DIRECTOR: Thomas Carr
CAST: Burgess Meredith, Patty McCormack, Arch Johnson, Peter Helm, Beau Bridges, Neil Nephew, Michael Davis

Favor and Jim cannot believe a rushing river is marked as a creek on their trail map. Two feuding ranchers do not realize the rising water is putting pressure on a dam and may flood the entire valley.

NOTES: No Mushy or Toothless despite a need for all the drovers. Beau Bridges is the son of the late Lloyd Bridges and brother of actor Jeff Bridges. This was the second *Rawhide* appearance by Patty McCormack, memorable as the evil child in both the stage and screen versions of *The Bad Seed* (1956).

#149: INCIDENT AT FARRAGUT PASS
(OCTOBER 31, 1963)

WRITER: Jack Turley
DIRECTOR: Thomas Carr
CAST: Frankie Avalon, Glenda Farrell, Tommy Farrell, John Pickard, William Henry, Ralph Reed, Dee Pollock

Wealthy landowner Elizabeth Farragut will not permit the drive to cross her land unless Favor hires her delinquent grandson and makes a man out of him.

NOTES: Nearly a Mushy vehicle. Despite the ordinary premise, one of the best episodes of the season: it features a surprisingly good performance by Frankie Avalon, best known for his Beach Party movies. The ending not entirely expected.

#150: INCIDENT AT TWO GRAVES
(NOVEMBER 7, 1963)

TELEPLAY: Al C. Ward & Samuel Roeca
STORY: Al C. Ward
DIRECTOR: Harry Harris
CAST: Bill Travers, Steve Brodie, Don Haggerty, Dennis Cross

Rowdy helps a bare knuckle fighter escape from an angry mob. The fighter is in possession of a gold and silver cross that Hey-Soos is part of the lost treasure of Los Padres.

NOTES: A grave marker indicates that the year is 1870. The fighter says Rowdy reminds him of his dead son. Another surprise ending.

#151: INCIDENT OF THE RAWHIDERS
(NOVEMBER 14, 1963)

TELEPLAY: Jack Turley & Jay Simms
STORY: Jay Simms
DIRECTOR: Ted Post
CAST: Denver Pyle, Nina Shipman, James Best, Wright King, John Mitchum

The drive is menaced by a band of rawhiders, and Rowdy is being forced to marry one of their women.

NOTES: Denver Pyle, who plays Daddy Quade, was the head of the Darling clan on *The Andy Griffith Show* and the father of no-good sons in "No Hands," a memorable episode of *Gunsmoke*. He guest starred on more than sixty television Westerns, including regular roles on *The Life and Legend of Wyatt Earp* and *The Life and Times of Grizzly Adams*. He won a Golden Boot Award in 1984 and died at the age of 77 in 1998. Wright King portrayed Steve McQueen's partner Jason for one season of *Wanted Dead or Alive*.

#152: Incident of the Prophecy
(November 21, 1963)

WRITER: Samuel Roeca
DIRECTOR: Thomas Carr
CAST: Dan Duryea, Warren Oates, James Griffith, Raymond
            Guth, Dean Stanton, Hugh Sanders, Ray Teal

Rowdy and drover Charlie "Rabbit" Walters take turns shooting at a church bell. A bullet ricochets and kills the brother of a deranged gunslinger who considers himself a preacher. He predicts that both Rowdy and the superstitious Walter are going to die.

NOTES: This episode was broadcast the night before the JFK assassination. Warren Oates guest starred on nearly forty Western series, in addition to co-starring on Jack Lord's *Stoney Burke*.

#153: Incident at Confidence Creek
(November 28, 1963)

WRITER: Jack Turley
DIRECTOR: Harry Harris
CAST: Dick York, Barbara Eden, Roy Roberts, Roy
            Barcroft, J. Pat O'Malley, Harry Lauter, Richard
            Wessel, Byron Foulger, Norman Leavitt

Wishbone makes the mistake of telling a pair of stranded entertainers all there is to know about the business end of a cattle drive. The two steal the ownership papers and plan to sell the herd, one of them posing as Favor.

NOTES: Sitcom veterans Dick York (*Bewitched*) and Barbara Eden (*I Dream of Jeannie*) each made two episodes of *Rawhide*. At the time, Eden was married to frequent *Rawhide* guest star Michael Ansara.

#154: Incident of the Death Dancer
(December 5, 1963)

WRITER: Dean Riesner
DIRECTOR: Thomas Carr
CAST: Forrest Tucker, Med Flory

Mushy is attacked by what the drovers assume is a puma. A man who has been hunting the cat for four years tells them it is an African lion that escaped from a train bound for Denver. According to the Pawnee, it cannot be killed.

NOTES: Usual fine performance by Forrest Tucker, who appeared on more than fifteen Westerns, but made only one *Rawhide*. He also co-starred on the comedy Westerns *F Troop* and *Dusty's Trail*. Med Flory was also very active in the genre, guest starring on nearly twenty series, including two episodes of *Rawhide*.

#155: INCIDENT OF THE WILD DEUCES
(DECEMBER 12, 1963)

TELEPLAY: Preston Wood & Jack Turley
STORY: Preston Wood
DIRECTOR: Harry Harris
CAST: Barbara Stuart, George Chandler, Ken Lynch,
               Robert B. Williams, William Henry,
               W.J. "Sailor" Vincent

Jim and Joe try to get on Mushy's good side when he wins over fifteen hundred dollars in a poker game. The money leads to nothing but trouble, so Mushy decides to try losing it in another game.

NOTES: Although he is usually rough on Mushy in front of the other drovers, Wishbone shows a caring side in private, telling him that extra money means extra responsibility, not extra things. "Don't put your trust in money—put your money in trust."

#156: INCIDENT OF THE GEISHA
(DECEMBER 19, 1963)

WRITER: Charles Larson
DIRECTOR: Ted Post
CAST: Miyoshi Umeki, Joseph Perry

On the way to get a doctor for Rowdy, Hey-Soos is knocked unconscious by a tree branch. When he comes to, he finds himself being cared for by a young Japanese woman.

Notes: Guest star Miyoshi Umeki won an Academy Award for her performance in 1957's *Sayonara*, whose cast included *Maverick*'s James Garner.

#157: Incident at Ten Trees
(January 2, 1964)

Teleplay: Carey Wilbur
Story: A.I. Bezzerides
Director: Ted Post
Cast: Susan Kohner, Royal Dano, Michael Pate, Iron
             Eyes Cody

Favor and Jim find a white woman dressed in Cheyenne garb suffering from shock. An Indian chief tells the drovers she is a witch who has brought bad luck to the tribe and must die.

Notes: One of the better episodes of the series. Though not listed in the credits, the Cheyenne medicine man is played by well-known Western actor Iron Eyes Cody.

#158: Incident of the Rusty Shotgun
(January 9, 1964)

Teleplay: Paul King
Story: Robert M. Stevens
Director: Ted Post
Cast: Claude Akins, Marie Windsor, Herbert Anderson,
             Don Megowan, Kelly Thordson, Jonathan Hole,
             Don Beddoe

Wishbone tells Mushy that living in a town would be paradise, but he changes his tune when three brothers decide he would make a perfect husband for their storekeeper sister.

Notes: Marie Windsor, awarded a Golden Boot in 1984, was deliberately de-glamorized for this episode, one of her three *Rawhide* appearances.

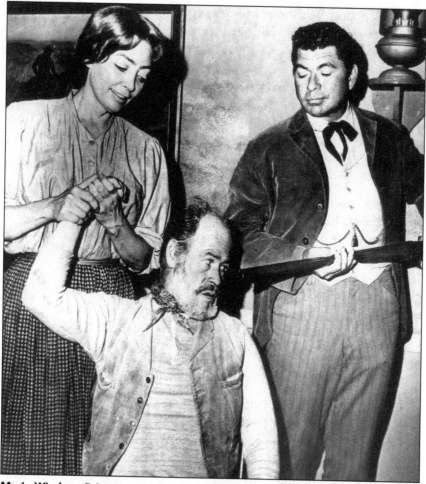

Marie Windsor, Brinegar and Claude Akins in "Incident of the Rusty Shotgun."

#159: INCIDENT OF MIDNIGHT CAVE
(JANUARY 16, 1964)

TELEPLAY: Barry Trivers & Samuel Roeca
STORY: Barry Trivers
DIRECTOR: Thomas Carr
CAST: Edward Kemmer

When the herd reaches high country, Wishbone admits to Rowdy that he has been wary of heights ever since he was young and older boys stranded him in a church belfry. He falls off a cliff and clings to some brush. After he is rescued, he goes in and out of consciousness, but when he finally comes to he cannot see.

NOTES: Second Wishbone episode in a row. Ed Kemmer appeared in over twenty different Western series.

#160: INCIDENT OF THE DOWERY DUNDEE
(JANUARY 23, 1964)

TELEPLAY: Samuel Roeca
STORY: Samuel Roeca & Joy Dexter
DIRECTOR: Ted Post
CAST: Hazel Court, Lyle Bettger

Rowdy and Jim are looking for strays when their horses are spooked by a big ox. A Scottish woman with three more oxen shoos the beast away and invites the drovers to join her for tea. It turns out she may be related to Mushy.

NOTES: Jim tells Rowdy this is his last drive: that he is going to buy a saloon when they get to Denver. Wishbone calls Mushy by his rightful name, Harkness. The word dowry is misspelled in the episode title.

#161: INCIDENT AT GILA FLATS
(JANUARY 30, 1964)

TELEPLAY: Paul King & Samuel Roeca
STORY: Samuel Roeca
DIRECTOR: Thomas Carr
CAST: Gene Evans, Leslie Wales, Harry Lauter, Rodolfo Acosta, Edward Faulkner, Med Flory, L.Q. Jones, Mike Ragan, Joseph Vitale, Michael Keep, Buck Holland

An army major wants two hundred head of Favor's herd as part of a treaty with the Apaches. Renegades from the tribe are determined to prevent the treaty from being signed.

NOTES: A suspenseful, fast paced episode. Edward Faulkner guest starred on more than fifteen Western series, including seven episodes of *Rawhide*.

Eastwood in "Incident of the Dowery Dundee."

#162: INCIDENT OF THE PIED PIPER
(FEBRUARY 6, 1964)

TELEPLAY:	Albert Aley & Samuel Roeca
STORY:	Albert Aley
DIRECTOR:	Harry Harris
CAST:	Eddie Bracken, Everett Sloane, Arch Johnson, Duane Grey, Rodney Bell, Butch Patrick, Jennie Lynn, Peter Bobbins, Christopher Barrey

A tornado kills forty cows and scatters hundreds more. The drovers spend several days rounding up the strays and discover that the head of an orphanage has been selling some of the cattle.

NOTES: Eddie Bracken's second guest appearance. Butch Patrick, who did several television Westerns, is better known as Eddie on *The Munsters*, which began later this same year.

#163: INCIDENT OF THE SWINDLER
(FEBRUARY 20, 1964)

TELEPLAY: John Hawkins & Jack Turley
STORY: Jack Turley
DIRECTOR: Thomas Carr
CAST: John Dehner, Sally Forrest, Peter Leeds, Richard
               Reeves, William Fawcett

A thief tries to steal a horse from the remuda, and then threatens to tell the drovers that there is a reward of fifteen thousand dollars on Wishbone's head unless the cook helps him escape.

NOTES: John Dehner, who did five episodes of *Rawhide*, guest starred on numerous television Westerns and played Paladin on the radio version of *Have Gun-Will Travel*. He died in 1992 at the age of seventy-six. William Fawcett appeared on more than fifty different series and was a regular on *Fury*.

#164: INCIDENT OF THE WANDERER
(FEBRUARY 27, 1964)

WRITER: Carey Wilbur
DIRECTOR: Christian Nyby
CAST: Nehemiah Persoff, Gregory Walcott

Before a freak storm hits, several of the drovers spot a strange figure standing on a rise. The rain stops as suddenly as it began, and a man wearing a cape and using a cane limps into camp, perfectly dry. He claims he can prevent a half breed renegade from being executed for a crime he did not commit.

NOTES: A well-written episode as well as the last of Gregory Walcott's five guest roles on the series.

#165: INCIDENT AT ZEBULON
(MARCH 5, 1964)

WRITER: Dean Riesner
DIRECTOR: Christian Nyby
CAST: Robert Cornthwaite, Patricia Huston, John
               Lupton, Ron Foster, Kelly Thordsen, Herbert
               Patterson

Masked vigilantes ride into camp and take drover Johnny Larkin to the town of Zebulon to stand trial for a crime Larkin insists he did not commit. When Favor tries to intercede, he is tied to a wagon wheel and whipped.

NOTES: When Wishbone asks Favor if he could have killed in cold blood, the trail boss replies, "We'll never know." Western veteran I. Stanford Jolley receives no on-screen credit. John Lupton co-starred with Michael Ansara in the ABC series *Broken Arrow*.

#166: INCIDENT AT HOURGLASS
(MARCH 12, 1964)

WRITER: John Hawkins
DIRECTOR: Christian Nyby
CAST: Jay C. Flippen, Elizabeth MacRae, John Anderson,
               Kent Smith, Russell Arms

Favor goes to an army reservation and asks that they delay blasting a pass shut to build a dam so he can get his herd through. While there, an officer's wife kills her secret lover and pins the crime on Favor.

NOTES: Episode largely a showcase for Fleming, who does an admirable job. Also impressive are familiar faces Jay C. Flippen and John Anderson. Elizabeth McCrae played Festus's girlfriend on several episodes of *Gunsmoke*. Victor French, best known as Michael Landon's co-star on *Little House on the Prairie* and *Highway to Heaven*, receives no billing.

#167: INCIDENT OF THE ODYSSEY
(MARCH 26, 1964)

TELEPLAY: Samuel Roeca
STORY: Samuel Roeca & Sheldon Stark
DIRECTOR: Thomas Carr
CAST: Mickey Rooney, Carole Matthews, Raymond Guth, John Pickard

Favor has been pushing the drive harder than usual to avoid another herd infected with hoof-in-mouth disease. Rowdy and Wishbone go to town for supplies and decide to get a bath. While they are soaking, a former circus performer steals Rowdy's boots.

NOTES: Rowdy tells Wishbone he is tired of Favor taking out his temper on the men, and is thinking of quitting. Favor pays off four drovers who quit even though it is his policy that no one gets paid until the drive is finished. Good job by Mickey Rooney, one of history's most gifted performers. Western actor Roy Jenson appears unbilled.

#168: INCIDENT OF THE BANKER
(APRIL 2, 1964)

WRITER: Chris Miller
DIRECTOR: Christian Nyby
CAST: Lola Albright, Allyn Joslyn, Virginia Gregg, Addison Richards, Adrienne Marden, Don Diamond

Favor is badly in need of funds for the drive, but the banker in Ashton Corners will not grant the loan unless he and the trail boss switch jobs.

NOTES: Favor says he cannot figure out why he keeps pushing cows "with a bunch of idiots." When he adds that he ought to up and quit, Rowdy replies that he should. Humorous performance by Fleming in a story written by his writing partner, Chris Miller.

#169: INCIDENT OF EL TORO
(APRIL 9, 1964)

WRITER: Charles Larson
DIRECTOR: Thomas Carr
CAST: James Best, Hal Baylor, John Cole, William
             Thompkins, Brad Morrow Jones

With the drovers a week behind schedule and Clay Forrester unsure of the trail ahead, the last thing the drive needs is the wild bull that is spooking the cattle. Hey-Soos says his brother was killed by a similar bull and that he wants to be the one to kill it.

NOTES: A leftover episode from either season four or five, copyright 1962, with old opening and Charles Gray as Clay Forrester in the cast.

#170: INCIDENT AT DEADHORSE—PART 1
(APRIL 16, 1964)

WRITER: Paul King
DIRECTOR: Thomas Carr
CAST: Burgess Meredith, Broderick Crawford, Chill
             Wills, Robert Middleton, Paul Carr, Hampton
             Fancher, Hugh Sanders, I. Stanford Jolley
             (uncredited)

On the way to Deadhorse, New Mexico, Rowdy and Jim discover a man buried alive under a pile of rocks. He turns out to be a hangman whose duty it is to execute the most prominent citizen of Deadhorse.

NOTES: First two-part episode of the series, and a good one in spite of the fact that the regulars take a backseat to the formidable guest cast. Eastwood guest starred on Broderick Crawford's *Highway Patrol* series in 1955.

#171: INCIDENT AT DEADHORSE—PART 2
(APRIL 23, 1964)

NOTES: According to the episode, the year is 1870. Script for the second part is even better than part one.

#172: INCIDENT OF THE GILDED GODDESS
(APRIL 30, 1964)

WRITER: Don Brinkley
DIRECTOR: Christian Nyby
CAST: Dina Merrill, Herbert Rudley, Robert J. Stevenson

A disheveled woman, Lisa Temple, walks down from the hills to where Wishbone and Mushy are setting up camp. She claims she was on her way to join her husband at Fort Bradley and was thrown from her horse. Rowdy knows her and suspects she is lying.

NOTES: Lisa says she has to get out of Texas and into New Mexico, though in previous episodes the drive is already in New Mexico. Dina Merrill later portrayed one of Eric Fleming's Mormon wives in "The Pursued," a two-part episode of *Bonanza* that proved to be Fleming's final performance.

#173: INCIDENT AT SEVEN FINGERS
(MAY 7, 1964)

TELEPLAY: John Hawkins
STORY: John Hawkins & John Dunkel
DIRECTOR: Christian Nyby
CAST: William Marshall, Harry Townes, Don Marshall,
                Keg Johnson, Hari Rhodes

A soldier steals Rowdy's horse and boots, but Rowdy takes a liking to the man and offers him a job with the drive no matter who is chasing him or why. Favor suspects that the soldier is a deserter.

NOTES: Only episode of the series to feature a flashback sequence. William Marshall, who sings while Hey-Soos accompanies him on guitar, also sang in a *Bonanza* episode ("Enter Thomas Bowers") which had aired less than one week before.

#174: INCIDENT OF THE PEYOTE CUP
(MAY 14, 1964)

WRITER: Dick Nelson
DIRECTOR: Thomas Carr

CAST: James Gregory, Pilar Seurat, Ted de Corsia,
         Richard Hale, Hal Jon Norman

Hey-Soos is captured by a strange tribe and forced to drink a potion that causes him to hallucinate. An Indian girl helps him return to the drive, but the next night he insists on going back to rescue her.

NOTES: A rather vague and confusing story with religious overtones. Weak ending to what is generally considered the last classic season of *Rawhide*.

SEASON SEVEN

#175: THE RACE
(SEPTEMBER 25, 1964)

WRITER: Robert Lewin
DIRECTOR: Bernard McEveety
CAST: Warren Oates, Emile Genest, William Bryant,
             L.Q. Jones

In Yellow River, Rowdy quits the drive. A cattle owner is looking for a trail boss, and Favor recommends Rowdy. They compete to see who can reach the railhead first.

NOTES: New opening with sculptured busts of Fleming, Eastwood and Brinegar as well as shots—with obvious stunt doubles—morphing into action figures of the trio. Now produced by Bernard L. Kowalksi and Bruce Geller, with both Rocky Shahan and Robert Cabal dropped from the cast. The saloon set is *Gunsmoke*'s Long Branch. When Rowdy says he is quitting, Favor responds, "Again?" Rowdy hires Wishbone and Mushy for his drive, Favor promotes Jim Quince to ramrod. Eastwood flubs at the end of the episode by saying North Dakota instead of South Dakota. John Pickard appears as the marshal but is not credited.

#176: THE ENORMOUS FIST
(OCTOBER 2, 1964)

WRITER: Sam Ross
DIRECTOR: Bernard L. Kowalski
CAST: Brenda Scott, Lee Van Cleef, Adam Williams,

James Anderson, Douglas Henderson, Barry
Atwater, Walter Mathews, Mark Slade

Defending himself, Favor gets into a fight with the father of four
children and accidentally kills him.

NOTES: Western veteran Lee Van Cleef's first appearance on the series,
though brief. Mark Slade co-starred as Blue on *The High Chaparral*
for three seasons.

#177: PINEY
(OCTOBER 9, 1964)

WRITER: Clyde Ware
DIRECTOR: Philip Leacock
CAST: Ed Begley, J.D. Cannon, Tom Reese, Lee Van
                Cleef, Elisha Cook, Robert Karnes, Victor Izay,
                Jerry Davis, Leonard Yorr

Favor is looking forward to meeting his friend Piney Kinney in
Collins, Texas, and hopes the old man has recovered from losing
his land to the bank. In the meantime, Piney and a gang of outlaws
are digging an underground tunnel from the saloon to the bank.

NOTES: The regulars are guest stars on their own show in this episode.
Director Leacock also became a producer on *Gunsmoke* this season.
In one scene, the shadow of a boom microphone can be seen above
Ed Begley's head.

#178: THE LOST HERD
(OCTOBER 16, 1964)

WRITER: Archie L. Tegland
DIRECTOR: Vincent McEveety
CAST: Harry Townes, Royal Dano, Paul Comi, Leo
                Gordon, Peter Bourne, Bill Williams

Favor carelessly loses his herd when they stampede over a cliff in
country known as the Devil's Patchwork. The bank will not loan him
money to pay the drovers, so he cashes in a bag of gold dust, but it
is not enough.

Fleming and Ed Begley in "Piney."

NOTES: Stories seem to be getting smaller, more intimate and psychological, with more emphasis on character than plot. Camerawork and lighting are more inventive than usual, shots more creatively composed. Brief flashback sequence, the second of the series.

#179: A MAN CALLED MUSHY
(OCTOBER 23, 1964)

WRITER: John Mantley
DIRECTOR: Michael O'Herlihy
CAST: Mike Kellin, Sandra Kerr, Margo, John Hubbard, John McLiam, Jonathan Kidd, Michael Pataki, Dawn Little Sky, Paul Comi

While the drovers load cattle into train cars in Silver Creek, Mushy allows gypsies to take the drive's wagons and horses, believing them when they say they have bought everything from Favor.

NOTES: One of the better episodes of the season, written by Mantley, a future *Gunsmoke* producer. No concentration on a single drive this year. Rowdy and Favor starting to butt heads more often. Another use of *Gunsmoke*'s Long Branch Saloon.

#180: CANLISS
(OCTOBER 30, 1964)

WRITER: Stirling Silliphant
DIRECTOR: Jack Arnold
CAST: Dean Martin, Laura Devon, Michael Ansara, Ramon Novarro, Stewart Moss, Teno Pollick, Rico Alaniz, Theodore Bikel, Jack Kruschen, Scott Marlowe

Hired gun Gurd Canliss wants to quit the violent life for his wife's sake, but agrees to one more job for fifteen hundred dollars.

NOTES: Rare dramatic television performance by Dean Martin, who was a huge fan of Westerns. Literate script by Silliphant, but the *Rawhide* cast is barely necessary for this episode. Rowdy does not appear at all. Music this season more varied than in the past, due to contributions from several different composers.

#181: DAMON'S ROAD—PART 1
(NOVEMBER 13, 1964)

WRITERS: Richard Carr & Robert Lewin
DIRECTOR: Michael O'Herlihy

Brinegar and Barbara Eden in "Damon's Road."

CAST: Fritz Weaver, Barbara Eden, Sean McClory, Robert Sorrells, Curt Conway, J. Edward McKinley, Stevan Darrell, Kitty Malone, Rita D'Amico, Beatrice Montiel, Paul Comi

A railroad boss whose crew has quit schemes to replace them with the Gil Favor outfit.

NOTES: Second and final two-part episode of the series. An unlikely opportunity for Fleming to show off his comedic skills. Song "Bet it Up, Boys" features music by Rudy Schrager and lyrics by producer Bruce Geller.

Barbara Eden and Eastwood in "Damon's Road."

#182: DAMON'S ROAD—PART 2
(NOVEMBER 20, 1964)

NOTES: Despite several amusing scenes, this special two-part episode is not very special. Favor says "Head 'em up, move 'em out!" twice within ten seconds. Lyrics to "Ten Tiny Toes" by Geller, music by Schrager.

#183: THE BACKSHOOTER
(NOVEMBER 27, 1964)

WRITER: Richard Carr
DIRECTOR: Herschel Daugherty
CAST: Louis Hayward, Slim Pickens, Holly McIntire, Terry Becker, Robert Yuro, Joseph Hoover, George Keymas, Steve Gravers, Roy Engel, Jan Arvan, Frank Maxwell

A wanted man asks Rowdy to turn him in and give the reward to his wife, but someone shoots the outlaw in the back. When Rowdy brings the body to Morgan City, everyone assumes he killed the man in such a cowardly manner.

NOTES: Slim Pickens, who died in 1983, guest starred on no less than forty different Western series, including regular roles on *The Outlaws* and *Custer*. He and Sheb Wooley made their big screen debuts together in Errol Flynn's *Rocky Mountain* (1950). This was Pickens' only episode of *Rawhide*.

#184: CORPORAL DASOVIK
(DECEMBER 4, 1964)

WRITER: Lionel L. Siegel
DIRECTOR: Bernard L. Kowalski
CAST: Nick Adams, John Drew Barrymore, Cyril Delevanti, Ron Soble, Barry Atwater, Howard Caine, Sherwood Price, John Dierkes

Army troopers shoot Favor in the leg after he fires on them for trying to steal two rare cows. The soldiers take him to their camp, where a young corporal agonizes over being left in charge of escorting a band of Utes to a reservation.

NOTES: Nick Adams starred as Johnny Yuma in the series *The Rebel*. He died less than four years after this episode aired. The late John Drew Barrymore, father of actress Drew Barrymore, specialized in portraying off-center characters, including his three appearances on *Rawhide*.

#185: THE PHOTOGRAPHER
(DECEMBER 11, 1964)

WRITER: Clyde Ware
DIRECTOR: Vincent McEveety
CAST: Eddie Albert, Ben Cooper, William O'Connell, Richard X. Slattery, Morgan Woodward, Frank Richards, Kelton Garwood

A photographer who once assisted the famous Matthew Brady has joined up with the drive, much to Favor's annoyance. Rowdy believes he is escorting the man to take pictures of a Shoshone medicine dance, but the real subject is a gang of outlaws.

NOTES: Eddie Albert's modern wristwatch is visible in one scene. The only *Rawhide* appearance by the versatile and dynamic Morgan Woodward, who recalls that the outlaw scenes were shot on the CBS Studio City lot, not on location. Woodward guest starred on more than thirty television Westerns and had a regular role on *The Life and Legend of Wyatt Earp*. He holds the record for appearing in more episodes of *Gunsmoke* and *Wagon Train* than any other guest star. Christopher Dark, who had the honor of being the first actor to be shot on *Bonanza*, is uncredited.

#186: NO DOGS OR DROVERS
(DECEMBER 18, 1964)

WRITERS: Sam Ross & Cliff Gould
DIRECTOR: Vincent McEveety
CAST: Philip Abbott, Paul Comi, Leonard Stone, Gilbert Green, Dabbs Greer, Barbara Baldovin, Eugene Borden, Bryan O'Byrne, John Zaremba, Zeme North

The drive reaches Junction City, and the outfit intends to whoop it up, but while Favor is given royal treatment by cattle owner Ben Dennis and the owner of the hotel, the townspeople give the drovers the cold shoulder.

NOTES: A rare seventh season installment featuring the regular cast instead of concentrating on guest stars. Mushy tells the other men they ought to go to Abilene to do their drinking because "they like us there." Character actor Olan Soule, who received billing in four other episodes of *Rawhide*, here is uncredited.

#187: The Meeting
(January 1, 1965)

WRITER: Robert Lewin
DIRECTOR: Michael O'Herlihy
CAST: Gavin MacLeod, Don Quine, Richard Karlan,
             Dean Stanton, Len Wayland, Mel Gallagher,
             John Hart, Ric Roman

Outlaws tell Favor and some other trail bosses that they intend to form a syndicate and take over the country's beef market. Favor pretends to go along with the idea.

NOTES: An unusual episode with a somewhat novel ending. Some sources erroneously give the air date as December 25, 1964. When Favor is asked about Rowdy, he replies, "That big, dumb kid? What you gonna say about him 'cept he's healthy." Not mentioning his daughters, Favor says he is single and has no ties. Don Quine co-starred on *The Virginian* for two seasons.

#188: The Book
(January 8, 1965)

WRITER: Cliff Gould
DIRECTOR: Bernard L. Kowalski
CAST: Pat Hingle, J.D. Cannon, Leonard Stone, Valentin
             de Vargus, Ziva Rodann, Malcom Atterbury,
             Robert Cleaves, Madelyn Darrow, Walter Edmiston,
             Victor Izay, Alan Roberts, Timothy Carey

Pop Starke, who arranges gunfights between selected men for perverse fun and profit, has his eye on Rowdy. He says the ramrod could make ten thousand a year if they become partners.

NOTES: Despite a lot of close-ups and fast cuts in the editing, a rather talky episode. A drover remarks that Rowdy almost has his own herd, but could do better.

Pat Hingle briefly took over as Dodge City's doctor while *Gunsmoke's* Milburn Stone recuperated from heart surgery in 1971.

#189: JOSH
(JANUARY 15, 1965)

WRITERS: Robert E. Thompson & Herschel Daugherty
CAST: Albert Dekker, Ann Shoemaker, John Doucette,
            J.C. Flippen, John Pickard, Ottola Nesmith,
            George Greco, Paul Comi

Favor fires an aging trail hand whom Mushy has befriended, then reconsiders. The old man has his pride, and later challenges Favor to a showdown.

NOTES: Mushy expects to get a letter from a gypsy girl he met in the episode "A Man Called Mushy." The old trail hand tells him to forget about the drive and go back to the girl. John Doucette was another fixture on the Western circuit, appearing on more than forty different series.

#190: A TIME FOR WAITING
(JANUARY 22, 1965)

WRITER: Sy Salkowitz
DIRECTOR: Charles Rondeau
CAST: George Grizzard, Lin McCarthy, Lisabeth Hush,
            Larry Ward, Ken Kerry, George Murdock, Arthur
            Malet, Michael Barrier, Don Paulin

Rowdy rides to Fort Mason, summoned by a captain who is about to be hanged because of the ramrod's testimony.

NOTES: The episode contains only the third flashback sequence in the history of the series.

#191: A MOMENT IN THE SUN
(JANUARY 29, 1965)

WRITER: Bernard Girard
DIRECTOR: Bernard Girard

CAST: Gene Evans, Billy Gray, Sherry Jackson, Karl
          Swenson, Pat Conway, Rayford Barnes, Noel
          Drayton, Donald Ein, Tyler McVey

Favor and Rowdy get mixed up with Reed McCuller, an outlaw generous to local farmers and townspeople whom no one but the marshal wants to see behind bars.

NOTES: Intervals of corny singing by musical duo Bud & Travis, who also sang the theme for the *Stagecoach West* series. The song "A Moment in the Sun" was written by Van McCoy and producer Bruce Geller. The cast is an unusual combination of former child actors (Billy Gray, Sherry Jackson) and Western veterans (Evans, Swenson, Conway, Barnes, McVey).

#192: TEXAS FEVER
(FEBRUARY 5, 1965)

WRITER: John Dunkel
DIRECTOR: Harmon Jones
CAST: Royal Dano, Judi Meredith, Frank Maxwell,
             Christopher Dark, Douglas Kennedy, Willard Sage,
             Duane Grey, Jacque Shelton

A rancher threatens Hey-Soos, whom he refers to as "Pedro." Pete Nolan tells the rancher to back off, and is later accused of murdering him.

NOTES: CBS, alarmed at *Rawhide*'s drop in the ratings under producers Geller and Kowalski, put Endre Bohem back in charge for this and eight other episodes. Also back were Sheb Wooley, Robert Cabal and Rocky Shahan, with no explanation as to where they had been. Writer Dunkel and director Jones, longtime *Rawhide* associates, wasted no time getting the show back on track. Opening from earlier season, with Sheb Wooley.

#193: BLOOD HARVEST
(FEBRUARY 12, 1965)

WRITER: Walter Black
DIRECTOR: Justus Addiss

CAST: Steve Forrest, Tom Tully, Michael Petit, Rayford Barnes, Michael Witney, Paul Bryar, Richard X. Slattery

The drive picks up a man and his son, who claim their horses were spooked and ran off, but Favor has his doubts. Meanwhile, two drovers conspire to steal Favor's bill of sale.

NOTES: No Rowdy in this episode, nor is Clint Eastwood listed in the credits. Tom Tully portrayed Rowdy's father in the episode "Rio Salado." Steve Forrest made several television Westerns, but only one *Rawhide*.

#194: THE VIOLENT LAND
(MARCH 5, 1965)

WRITER: Buckley Angell
DIRECTOR: Harmon Jones
CAST: Davey Davison, Michael Forest, Gregg Palmer, Jacque Shelton, Lew Brown, Paul Sorenson, Julia Montoya

Pete returns to camp bedraggled and bearing bad news: two bands of Mescalero Apaches are in the area. He spots a new drover whom he recognizes as a Comanchero, and asks Favor when the drive started hiring rats.

NOTES: The drive arrives at a burned down ranch with three graves, one of them Rowdy's sister, who "practically raised" him. Gregg Palmer guest starred on more than fifty different Western series.

#195: THE WINTER SOLDIER
(MARCH 12, 1965)

WRITER: John Dunkel
DIRECTOR: Justus Addiss
CAST: Robert Blake, Brooke Bundy, Jim Boles, Liam Sullivan, Robert Bice, Stanley Clements, Ralph Reed, Dennis Cross, James Jeter

Afraid of Comanches, Hap Johnson deserts the army and hides out with the Gil Favor outfit. When soldiers find his horse among the remuda, they accuse Hey-Soos of helping the man escape.

NOTES: Return of the secondary theme song "Beyond the Sun." Hap claims his mother knew Wishbone's mother in Texas.

#196: PRAIRIE FIRE
(MARCH 19, 1965)

TELEPLAY: Elliott Arnold & Louis Vittes
STORY: Elliott Arnold
DIRECTOR: Jesse Hibbs
CAST: Michael Conrad, Anthony Caruso, Hal Baylor, John Hart, Jacque Shelton, John Boyer, Vic Perrin

Wishbone promises Todd Murdoch, a dying friend from his mountain man days, that he will make sure that the money from a cattle sale goes to Murdoch's daughter. Murdoch's hired men have other plans, and abduct Wishbone.

NOTES: Yet another welcome return to the show's original flavor, with John Hart back as drover Narbo. Mushy gets a chance to drive cattle instead of washing dishes. In a letter, Wishbone purposely addresses Favor as Gil, which Rowdy considers strange.

#197: RETREAT
(MARCH 26, 1965)

WRITER: John Dunkel
DIRECTOR: James Goldstone
CAST: John Anderson, Steve Ihnat, Ford Rainey, John Lasell, Keith McConnell, Jacque Shelton, Jan Arvan

Major Cantwell, on the verge of retirement, steals the army payroll and hides it in a package he asks Favor to mail for him. Another soldier rides off with the package, pursued by Cantwell and Favor.

NOTES: A Geller/Kowalski production, but a good script by *Rawhide* veteran Dunkel.

#198: THE EMPTY SLEEVE
(APRIL 2, 1965)

TELEPLAY: Louis Vittes
STORY: Endre Bohem
DIRECTOR: Justus Addiss
CAST: Everett Sloane, Burt Douglas, Dick Davalos, John Pickard, David Manley, Don Kennedy, Nancy Rennick

When the herd refuses to drink, Rowdy consults a veterinarian who says the cattle have been eating burned out grass that has no minerals. The cows need salt. Favor orders a one-armed drover to take the drive's wagons to a town with a salt mine, but the man is reluctant to go.

NOTES: Another episode produced by Bohem, who also contributed the story. No Mushy; Hey-Soos helping Wishbone with the cooking.

#199: THE LAST ORDER
(APRIL 9, 1965)

WRITER: Tom Seller
DIRECTOR: Robert L. Friend
CAST: Efrem Zimbalist, Jr., Lawrence Dobkin, Harry Lauter, Kelton Garwood, Rex Holman, Bruce Mars, Ken Konopka

Wishbone shoots one of the outlaws who steal a strongbox containing thousands of dollars from a stagecoach. That night, the wounded man staggers into camp with the box and dies.

NOTES: A Bohem-produced episode. Mushy asks Wishbone if a new hat will make him look like "a man of the world." Wishbone tells him he needs a new head.

#200: MRS. HARMON
(APRIL 16, 1965)

WRITER: John Mantley
DIRECTOR: Michael O'Herlihy
CAST: Barbara Barrie, Paul Lambert, Jim Hampton,

Pat Cardi, William Wintersole, Richard O'Brien

Following a boy who he sees steal a sack of flour, Wishbone discovers a woman beaten by her husband, a drunk Rowdy has refused to hire.

NOTES: A Geller/Kowalski episode, with another good script by John Mantley. Wishbone once again says he is tired of jokes about his cooking and beard, as well as grease burns.

#201: THE CALF WOMEN
(APRIL 30, 1965)

TELEPLAY: Louis Vittes & Buckley Angell
STORY: Buckley Angell
DIRECTOR: Tony Leader
CAST: Julie Harris, Kelly Thordsen, Karl Lukas, John Boyer, Betty Conner, Roger Ewing

The drive runs into buffalo hunters who do not want the cattle running off the buffalo. Mushy cannot bring himself to shoot the calves Wishbone has told him to kill, but two sisters say they will take them to their ranch.

NOTES: Another Bohem episode. No Favor and no mention of Fleming in the credits. Rowdy temporary trail boss, Jim Quince reluctant ramrod. Final episode with Robert Cabal as Hey-Soos. Dramatic television debut of Julie Harris, perhaps best known for co-starring with James Dean in *East of Eden*. Roger Ewing portrayed Thad Greenwood on two seasons of *Gunsmoke*.

#202: THE SPANISH CAMP
(MAY 7, 1965)

WRITER: John Dunkel
DIRECTOR: Harmon Jones
CAST: Brock Peters, John Ireland, Rico Alaniz, John Erwin

Dr. Joseph Merritt and his crew are searching for treasure, and their digging has cut off the water supply for Favor's herd. When

Julie Harris and Eastwood in "The Calf Women."

Wishbone is injured, Merritt refuses to help, saying he has vowed never to practice medicine again.

NOTES: End of an era: Last appearances of Rocky Shahan as Joe Scarlett and Sheb Wooley as Pete Nolan, first appearance of John Erwin as Teddy after a long absence. Also the last of the nine episodes in season seven produced by Endre Bohem. John Ireland would join the cast the next season.

#203: EL HOMBRE BRAVO
(MAY 14, 1965)

WRITER: Herman Groves
DIRECTOR: Philip Leacock
CAST: Frank Silvera, Malachi Throne, Manuel Padilla,
             Henry Corden, Carmelita Acosta

In Mexico, Favor and Mushy are driving some prize cattle to Kansas when they are stopped by men looking for a revolutionary named El Hombre Bravo. Later, the drovers encounter the man, who is actually a school teacher leading a group of children out of harm's way.

NOTES: Although in the desert, Favor wears no hat. Frank Silvera portrayed Don Sebastian Montoya on *The High Chaparral*. Manuel Padilla played Jai on NBC's *Tarzan* series.

#204: THE GRAY ROCK HOTEL
(MAY 21, 1965)

WRITER: Jack Curtis
DIRECTOR: Stuart Rosenberg
CAST: Steven Hill, Lola Albright, Strother Martin,
             Vic Tayback, Rex Holman (uncredited)

All the drovers but Favor have come down with some kind of sickness. They hole up in a ghost town's hotel, and are confronted by a man-hating woman holding a gun on them.

NOTES: Guest stars Hill and Albright listed before all other opening credits. Moody, Western noir. Rare opportunity for James Murdock to display a more dramatic side in his final appearance as Mushy. Rowdy tells Favor he feels "Rowdy" in name only. Outstanding character actor Strother Martin's part is criminally brief. Eric Fleming's last episode.

SEASON EIGHT

#205: ENCOUNTER AT BOOT HILL
(SEPTEMBER 14, 1965)

WRITER: Anthony Spinner
DIRECTOR: Sutton Roley
CAST: Simon Oakland, Jeff Corey, Peter Haskell, Malcom
              Atterbury, Timothy Carey, David Watson

Two drovers are shot, one fatally, while trying to prevent a hanging. Rowdy, Jim and new drovers Simon and Ian ride into town to report the killing only to find justice in short supply.

NOTES: The series now produced by Ben Brady and Robert E. Thompson. New opening with sketches of Western characters and a re-recording of the familiar theme. *Rawhide* logo no longer in rustic lettering. No explanation of where Simon Blake and Ian Cabot have come from, or why Rowdy is now trail boss, and Jim Quince ramrod. And not one head of cattle in sight.

#206: RIDE A CROOKED MILE
(SEPTEMBER 21, 1965)

TELEPLAY: N.B. Stone, Jr. & Herman Miller
STORY: N.B. Stone, Jr.
DIRECTOR: Justus Addiss
CAST: John Drew Barrymore, Douglas Kennedy,
              Harry Lauter

The drive's new scout, Jed Colby, rides in with Danny Hawks, who says he will be glad to work only for his keep, no pay. Rowdy agrees to take him on, but Simon has seen Hawks before and knows he is "pure trouble."

NOTES: John Ireland's first episode as Jed Colby. Never explained where he came from, but this would have been a much better season opener.

#207: SIX WEEKS TO BENT FORK
(SEPTEMBER 28, 1965)

WRITER: Mort R. Lewis
DIRECTOR: Thomas Carr
CAST: James Gregory, R.G. Armstrong, L.Q. Jones, David
               Watson, Vaughn Taylor, Roy Roberts (uncredited)

A cattleman says he will pay Rowdy's outfit a handsome bonus if they can get his herd to market in six weeks, but he will pay them nothing if they do not. He insists that his top hand accompany the drive, which leads to friction.

NOTES: An episode almost on par with the old classics, but Fleming and the other former cast members are missed. Dates superimposed on calendar are May and June 1872. Roy Roberts, who appears unbilled, often played the banker on *Gunsmoke*. L.Q. Jones is introduced as drover P.J. Peters.

#208: WALK INTO TERROR
(OCTOBER 5, 1965)

TELEPLAY: Joanna Thompson & Jerry Adelman
STORY: Jerry Adelman
DIRECTOR: Thomas Carr
CAST: Claude Akins, Jerry Boggs, Bruce Dern, Ed
               Rankin, Roy Barcroft

Jim and Simon scout for the best way through an old coal mining site. When they enter the mine, Jim is attacked by a bear. Simon shoots at it, and the mine caves in.

NOTES: The only *Rawhide* by guest star Bruce Dern, who appeared

Raymond St. Jacques, David Watson, Eastwood, Steve Raines and Brinegar.

on nearly fifteen different series and will be forever known to Western fans as the man who killed John Wayne in *The Cowboys*. Dern once said of his early career, "When your agent told you 'you're going to do a *Wagon Train*,' you *did* a *Wagon Train*." The phony bear costume is one of the worst in the history of the medium.

#209: Escort to Doom
(October 12, 1965)

WRITER: Walter Black
DIRECTOR: Alan Crosland
CAST: Rip Torn, Christopher Dark, Tom Reese,
            David Watson

Hoping to avoid trouble, Rowdy offers cattle and jobs to a band of Chiricahua Apaches that are following the herd. Their leader, a half-breed named Jacob, says his men are not women who drive cattle. The drovers and Indians enter an uneasy truce, but one warrior is determined to stampede the herd and kill the white men.

NOTES: One of the better episodes of the final season, mistakenly referred to as "Escape to Doom" in some sources. Wishbone reveals that he was only nine-years-old when one of his brothers was killed in a Chiricahua raid.

#210: Hostage for Hanging
(October 19, 1965)

WRITER: Walter Black
DIRECTOR: Herman Hoffman
CAST: Mercedes McCambridge, Warren Oates, Robert
            Blake, Sharon Farrell, Hal Baylor (uncredited)

Rowdy gives a woman and her sons a one hundred dollar deposit toward horses the drive needs. When he decides the horses are worthless and asks for the money back, one son knocks him out. The family demands three thousand dollars ransom from the drovers—or they will hang Rowdy.

NOTES: Ninth *Rawhide* for Hal Baylor, though he is not billed at the end of the episode.

#211: The Vasquez Woman
(October 26, 1965)

WRITERS: Boris Ingster & Louis Vittes
DIRECTOR: Bernard McEveety

Eastwood as Trail Boss.

CAST: Cesar Romero, Carol Lawrence,
Malachi Throne

Mexican Colonel Emilio Vasquez offers to buy cattle from the drive, but Jed tells him they are not for sale. Vasquez says he needs the cattle for a revolution, and at gunpoint gives the drovers forty thousand pesos, which Jed says will be worthless if there is another regime change in Mexico.

NOTES: A John Ireland episode, but arguably the weakest moment of the final season. No Rowdy. Jim refers to the pesos as "flour sack coupons." Victor French plays a bartender, not credited.

#212: Clash at Broken Bluff
(November 2, 1965)

TELEPLAY:	Louis Vittes
STORY:	Louis Vittes & Ed Adamson
DIRECTOR:	Charles Larson
CAST:	Ron Randell, Nancy Gates, Warren Stevens, David Watson, L.Q. Jones, Elizabeth Fraser, Lyn Edgington

Jim says the Webster spread will be a good place to keep the herd out of the wind, but that the owner, the biggest rancher in the territory, will charge a high price. Mrs. Webster tells them her husband has been dead for three years, and that they cannot use her land.

NOTES: The dead rancher's name was Jake, but Steve Raines slips and calls him Matt. Rowdy says he had a stepmother he did not like and was relieved when she died. Only *Rawhide* appearance by busy character actor Warren Stevens, guest star on more than twenty Western series. Music by Billy May, who frequently collaborated with Frank Sinatra.

#213: The Pursuit
(November 9, 1965)

WRITER:	John Dunkel
DIRECTOR:	Justus Addiss
CAST:	Ralph Bellamy, Jim Davis

The drive is stalked by a sniper, an elderly lawman from Missouri who claims Jed is a wanted man.

NOTES: Even a routine *Rawhide* like this one is enjoyable in comparison with the majority of the last episodes. Fine work by Ralph Bellamy and Jim Davis, both making their second and final appearances on the series.

#214: Duel at Daybreak
(November 16, 1965)

TELEPLAY: Robert Bloomfield & Herman Miller
STORY: Robert Bloomfield
DIRECTOR: Sutton Roley
CAST: Charles Bronson, Jill Haworth,
                 Larry Gates, Brendon Boone

A ranch foreman is trying to force one of the drovers into a gunfight. Jed recognizes the foreman as professional gunslinger Del Lingman, who cannot be beaten.

NOTES: Episode done strictly on the cheap, with back lot sets, phony exteriors, stock shots and no music credit. Teaser includes footage from 1958, in which a younger Eastwood can be briefly spotted. Large ranch house better known as the Barkley mansion from *The Big Valley*. Effective job, however, by guest star Bronson.

#215: Brush War at Buford
(November 23, 1965)

WRITER: Mort R. Lewis
DIRECTOR: Thomas Carr
CAST: Robert Middleton, Richard Carlson,
                 Skip Homeier, Tim McIntire, Robert Sorrells,
                 Harry Lauter, Mort Mills (uncredited)

The drive becomes trapped between two feuding ranchers who are still fighting the Civil War.

NOTES: Drago Santee is played by Mort Mills, guest star on more than forty different Western series, yet is uncredited in this, his only episode of *Rawhide*. He co-starred on the syndicated series *Man Without a Gun* (1957-59). The late Tim McIntire was the son of John McIntire, who replaced Ward Bond on *Wagon Train* and Charles Bickford on *The Virginian*.

#216: THE TESTING POST
(NOVEMBER 30, 1965)

WRITER: John Hawkins & Ward Hawkins
DIRECTOR: Gerd Oswald
CAST: Rory Calhoun, Burt Brinckerhoff, Dick Foran,
             Eddie Firestone, Robert Donner

When Rowdy wounds an army officer who tries to forcibly requisition some cattle at a below market price, Wishbone and Jed are worried that the ramrod has declared war between the army and all of the drovers.

NOTES: Good script by the Hawkins brothers, frequent contributors to *Bonanza*. Rory Calhoun starred in and co-produced *The Texan* for two seasons on CBS.

#217: CROSSING AT WHITE FEATHER
(DECEMBER 7, 1965)

WRITER: Robert Bloomfield
DIRECTOR: Richard Whorf
CAST: Albert Dekker, Johnny Crawford, G.B. Atwater,
             David Watson

Rowdy fires a drunken old timer, Jonas Bolt, who is the only person who knows how to get across a river filled with quicksand and potholes.

NOTES: Final episode of the series, directed by Richard Whorf, who also directed the first, "Incident of the Tumbleweed." Rowdy tells Bolt, "I knew someone just like you once" in reference to his father. Later, he tells Bolt's son that he is not sure where Dan Yates is, although he knows he is dead ("Rio Salado"). Rowdy shouts a variation of the famous "Head 'em up, move 'em out!" Johnny Crawford spent five seasons playing Mark McCain on *The Rifleman*.

INTERVIEW WITH
GREGORY WALCOTT

A ctor Gregory Walcott's career in film and television spanned five decades, from *Red Skies of Montana* (1952) to *Ed Wood* (1994). Some of his more prominent credits include *Battle Cry, Texas Lady,* the infamous *Plan 9 from Outer Space, The Outsider, Captain Newman, M.D., The Sugarland Express, Midway* and *Norma Rae*. In addition, he appeared in *Joe Kidd, Thunderbolt and Lightfoot, The Eiger Sanction* and *Every Which Way But Loose*, all with Clint Eastwood.

On television he portrayed Detective Roger Havilland in the 1961-62 NBC series *87th Precinct*. While he has guest starred on such varied programs as *Perry Mason, Dennis the Menace, The Mod Squad, Barnaby Jones, Dallas and Murder, She Wrote*, he left his biggest impression on the video range. His credits there are staggering: *Stories of the Century, Zane Grey Theatre, Sugarfoot, Frontier Doctor, 26 Men, Trackdown, Maverick, The Rifleman, Wichita Town, Tombstone Territory, Texas John Slaughter, The Tall Man, The Life and Legend of Wyatt Earp, Riverboat, Wagon Train, Tales of Wells Fargo, Bat Masterson, The Deputy, Laramie, The Dakotas, A Man Called Shenandoah, Shane, The Big Valley, Daniel Boone, The High Chaparral, Alias Smith and Jones, Bonanza, The Cowboys, Little House on the Prairie, The Quest* and five episodes of *Rawhide*.

Q: Did you enjoying watching all five of those *Rawhides* I sent?

A: Oh, yes, I did.

Q: Did you have any of them already?

A: No, and you know what's so amazing is that it's been more than thirty years, so be ready to kick in some names or questions that will help my memory.

Q: You did five episodes, and I think of the major character actors only Claude Akins did more. He did seven. You're number two. And you were in four of the eight seasons, including season six, which a lot of fans consider the last solid season. That was the episode you did with Nehemiah Persoff. But the first was "Incident in the Garden of Eden" with John Ireland and Debra Paget. Do you have any specific memories of that, now that you've seen it again?

A: I remember that I had a crush on her, prior to that. She was a very pretty girl, a very pretty lady. I liked her all the way back to when she had a contract with Fox.

Q: Do you have any other memories, after seeing the tape?

A: What struck me immediately was that my hair was darker, and the reason for that is that Charles Marquis Warren had an aversion to blonde cowboys. He'd always get me to darken my hair when I came on the show. In fact, he was the original producer on *Gunsmoke*, and he told me that he got Jim Arness to darken his hair. He just didn't like cowboys with blonde hair.

Q: You hair was really dark in the episode "Incident of the Gallows Tree," the one with Beverly Garland.

A: That's right, I remember that.

Q: Let's go back to that first episode, the one you did with John Ireland. He did another episode after that, and then became a regular on the series in its last year. What was he like to work with?

Gregory Walcott (COURTESY OF GREGORY WALCOTT).

A: He was not indifferent, he was not distant. He was just kind of quiet, very professional. It seemed like he came to work prepared. I didn't have a lot to do with him, and I don't remember a whole lot about that.

Q: Do you remember exactly where the exteriors were filmed?

A: We did a lot at MGM, but out in the wilds, that was out here in Thousand Oaks, which is now a lot of houses, all houses, about five miles from where I live now.

Q: The next one you did was "Incident at Poco Tiempo," with Agnes Moorehead.

A: Yes, I remember that one pretty well.

Q: That was one you said you had never seen, right?

A: That's right, not until you sent it to me, and I enjoyed watching that. That brought back several memories. I remember Agnes Moorehead had played all through the years as kind of a character actor, and she always played down her looks to make her look haggard, just kind of old and unpleasant. But she played a nun in this show, and I had scenes with her and noticed that she had lovely skin. Actually, I thought right then that she was rather pretty. And I was happy several years later, when she was on *Bewitched*, they glamorized her. I was glad she had the chance to look pretty, and she did. I was impressed with her. Good actress. She was very nice to me.

Q: They didn't use you for season four, but season five you were in twice.

A: Well, I'll tell you the reason why was because I was doing my TV series, *The 87th Precinct*, so I was gone for a couple of years and didn't do any shows except my own.

Q: "The Incident of the Hunter," with Mark Stevens and Hal Baylor, is the one where you get to shoot Clint Eastwood in the stomach.

A: Right in the belly. No, I didn't remember that one, which is strange. I usually remember those things.

Q: Yeah, you shoot Clint and ride off, and the other drovers go after you and drag you back. It's funny, because in one scene, where Eastwood's on the ground, if you look carefully you can see a shoeprint, and it looks like it's from a sneaker. One of the crew members must have been walking around there.

Q: What about "The Gallows Tree," with Beverly Garland?

A: Not long after that, she was a guest on one of the *Precinct* shows. I liked her. She was a good gal, very professional, very prepared.

Q: That's the one where your hair is really dark.

A: Yes, and a mustache.

Q: That's the one where they're going to hang Jim Quince, Steve Raines.

A: I remember doing that one, but not much about it. After all, it's been thirty-five, forty years.

Q: Yeah, that aired in 1963.

A: Oh, my!

Q: I asked Claude Akins about something specific once, and he said he'd done so much television that it was all a blur.

A: Yeah, yeah.

Q: What was Steve Raines like to work with? He always seemed like quite a character. He was the only one besides Eastwood and Paul Brinegar who stayed with the show all eight years.

A: He was a pleasant chap, just fun to talk to. Had a lot of stories to tell, just real easy to be with. I liked him very much.

Q: He was also a stunt rider.

A: Really? I didn't know.

Q: He also helped write a script.

A: He did? Did they use it?

Q: Yeah, they did.

A: You're kidding.

Q: No, I'm not. Even Eric Fleming wrote a couple. But I want to ask you about Ed Faulkner, who was also in "The Gallows Tree." He attends a lot of Western festivals. Did you ever get to know him very well?

A: Just briefly. I think he and I are going to be at a film festival in Williamsburg, Virginia, in March. I don't go to many of them anymore because, you know, I'm no spring chicken. But when they fly you in and put you up in a first class hotel, they want to use you, and that can wear me out. I enjoy it, though. But I get a little tired after a while.

Q: The reason I ask about Ed Faulkner is that I have a friend who's a shirttail relative of his, and he says they're both related to the writer William Faulkner. You might ask Ed about that. Anyway, you were also in season six, which a

lot of people consider the last really good year. You did
"Incident of the Wanderer" with Nehemiah Persoff.

A: Yes, yes, I'm glad you sent me that one because I really like
Nehemiah's performance in that, particularly in my death
scene. I particularly liked that, and I remember he was just
so tender. I even felt sorry for him, he held me so tenderly,
feeling remorseful, and I remember he did such a good job.
I was honored to work with him. He had a pretty good
stage background when he was in New York. I haven't seen
him lately.

Q: That was in February '64, and a lot of people consider
that the tail end of the good years.

A: That was when they had transferred over to the old
Republic Studios.

Q: They started out at Universal, then they went to MGM,
and *Rawhide* was the first show to move onto the Republic
lot when CBS bought it.

A: Oh, really?

Q: Did you ever get to know Sheb Wooley?

A: No, I never did too well. I had worked with him prior to
Rawhide, just here and there, but I didn't have any real
deep friendship with him. I just remember him around the
lot, hanging out with the other guys. But he was a nice
guy, pleasant guy.

Q: How about Rocky Shahan?

A: You know, I don't remember who Rocky Shahan is.

Q: He played Joe Scarlett. He never had too much to do on
the show, but he was on there for six years. He was more

of a stunt person who did some acting, like over on *Wagon Train*, Frank McGrath. He was a stunt person for John Ford.

A: Oh, yeah, I remember Frank.

Q: How about Robert Cabal, who played Hey-Soos. Any memories of him?

A: I don't have any memories of him.

Q: He kind of dropped out of sight. He did a *Big Valley*, and then not much was known about him until it was revealed recently that he died not too many years ago. The same is true of James Murdock, who played Mushy.

A: Was that the young boy?

Q: Yeah. He played kind of a simpleton.

A: Yeah, I remember him well because he kind of took up with me, always wanted to talk. But he was, like you said, kind of simple, quiet. He was impressed, I think, with older men, so I talked to him. In fact, one time he went to church with me one Sunday. He came over and went to church with me and my wife. That was the First Baptist Church of Beverly Hills.

Q: Do you know if he had a family or anything? I know he was from Illinois.

A: I don't know, but I would like to know.

Q: He had a couple minor roles on *Have Gun-Will Travel* and *Trackdown*, and then after *Rawhide* he did a *Gunsmoke* and *The Monroes*, and then he died of pneumonia on Christmas Eve, at quite a young age, in 1981.

A: He did? My, my, I didn't know that.

Q: In an interview one time, Paul Brinegar kind of suggested that maybe Murdock wasn't much brighter than the character he played. Did you get that impression?

A: Kind of. He did seem very simple, but he seemed nice. He didn't seem dumb.

Q: Not much is known about him.

A: Well, I'm sorry to hear that he passed away so young.

Q: Practically everyone who worked on the show is gone except Charles Gray. I'm going to be talking to him again. He and I have been corresponding. Of course, he played Clay Forrester. Had kind of a pencil-thin mustache.

A: That's right. He was kind of a leading man type. I don't think I ever had many scenes with him.

Q: He was brought on to take Sheb Wooley's place. I don't know how well you're familiar with the history, but it was sort of a rollercoaster. Sheb left, then he came back for an episode, then he left again. And then this other producer, Bruce Geller, who did *Mission: Impossible*, took over for one year and kind of ruined the show. So toward the end of the season, CBS brought Endre Bohem back, and he brought back all the cast members that this other producer had fired, including Sheb Wooley, to try to inject some life into the show.

A: Endre Bohem, yes, I certainly do remember him.

Q: Needless to say, Paul Brinegar was a character, wasn't he?

A: He sure was, oh, yes. Likeable, very much.

Q: What were your impressions of Eric Fleming? I've heard many different accounts of what he was like.

A: Distant. He and Clint would laugh a little bit, but I'd ride in a car with him, and he'd sit in the front seat and wouldn't say a word. He just seemed distant. Not really pleasant. He was kind of like the character he played on the show. I got along with him all right. I just didn't try to have fellowship with him. I wouldn't buy a *Time* magazine and sit there and read when we were going to work. He was kind of hard to get to know. He didn't show much interest in other people, or so it seemed.

Q: He had a really terrible childhood.

A: I didn't know that.

Q: He was terribly disfigured when a block of steel hit him in the face when he was in the Navy, but he said he didn't mind because he thought he looked better after the plastic surgery.

A: I didn't know that.

Q: Well, as you do know, he could be difficult to deal with, and then the producers used you as sort of tool to get him back in line, didn't they?

A: That was probably the biggest disappointment in my career in Hollywood. I had done several of the *Rawhides*, and it seemed like Charles Marquis Warren liked me. He had me come in and talk sometime, and he was very likeable. It seemed like he was kind of taking me under his arm, you know? So when the subject came up that Eric Fleming had walked off the show, Warren said he was going to use me as a replacement. But he said to me that since he had to get the approval of CBS, he had to do a test to show them that I looked good in the part. And he arranged a screen test, and he supervised the wardrobe, supervised the makeup, and he himself directed the screen test. There were about four or five short tests that he did to show me to the network in several different motifs. Anyway, he did these tests, and the whole crew was there, except Clint. Well done screen test, beautifully done, so when I walked away that day, I thought, "Well, I've got this one in the bag." It just felt that good. Then a few days went by, a week went by, and we didn't hear anything. So I called my agent and asked what was going on, and he said, "Well, I hate to tell you this, but Eric Fleming came back to the show." Then, about four years later, I went on an interview at Universal, where Charles Marquis Warren was a producer for *The Virginian*. He was in there with a director and two or three of his associates, and I came in for a reading or whatever it was, and he began to tell the story of having me do the test for *Rawhide*. And he laughed, he slapped his leg, he was so amused, he thought it was so clever that he had pulled this ruse on me and Eric Fleming. So the whole thing was that he went to a great deal of expense—it was even in the trade papers—just to convince Eric Fleming that he really was serious about replacing him with me. All this time it was just a joke, a ruse.

Q: Did he apologize?

A: Oh, no, no, he didn't. He didn't apologize at all. But Endre Bohem seemed to feel badly about it. He didn't apologize, he just seemed to feel badly about it. And one day he called me and said he liked the *Rawhide* test, and said he'd be glad to give me a copy he had there. So I got a copy from Endre Bohem, a very nice little man.

Q: Was Paul Brinegar in the test with you?

A: Yeah, he was there, just doing like he was supposed to, like I was a real star. He was very supportive, very helpful.

Q: You didn't have to audition for every episode, did you? They already knew your work.

A: Didn't have to audition for any of them.

Q: I don't know why CBS couldn't have just looked at one of your episodes instead of making you do a screen test.

A: Well, I think Charles Marquis Warren just wanted to show that he was very serious, and he went to all that trouble and all that expense, just to show them. But I'd have to say, again, that it was one of the biggest disappointments of my career.

Q: At the time you tested, that was one of the better Westerns on the air.

A: Yes, oh yes, definitely. By the way, do you know an actress who worked on that show, Jan Shepard? She was in that *Rawhide* screen test with me.

Q: She did three episodes.

A: Yeah, Jan and I went to school together early in my career, when I first came to California. She's a sweet girl, a real nice lady. We see her and her husband occasionally. They came to our fiftieth wedding anniversary. She was part of the test with me, we had a kissing scene, and she was very convincing.

Q: Do you and she still get a laugh out of that when you reminisce?

A: Oh, yes!

Q: Do you remember anything about Vincent Fennelly, when he took over the show?

A: No, I don't think I ever met him.

Q: You did some episodes when he was in charge, but a lot of times the producers don't come down to the set. Not like David Dortort did on *Bonanza*.

A: Oh, yes, wonderful David Dortort!

Q: How about Clint Eastwood, whom you've worked with many times?

A: Clint is a very nice person, very low key.

Q: You must have gotten quite a kick out of working with him and Robert Duvall in *Joe Kidd*.

A: Oh, yeah.

Q: Did Clint ask for you specifically for all those?

A: The feature films? Oh, yeah. In fact, when I was cast in *Every Which Way But Loose*, Marty Ritt wanted me for *Norma Rae*, Clint said he'd shoot around me so I could do both.

Q: Now that's a friend.

A: Yes, he is a friend. I thought that was very wonderful. Clint was the one who sponsored me to get into the Academy Awards. We were over in Switzerland doing *The Eiger Sanction*, and we got around to talking about the Oscars. I told him I wasn't a member of the Academy, and he said I should be, I had some good credits. He said, "I'll take care of that."

Q: Do you have any final memories of working on *Rawhide*?

A: Well, first of all I want to thank you for sending those episodes to me because they really add to my library, my collection. I really appreciate that. But I think maybe my main memory is the fact that I felt like I was abandoned or betrayed by Charles Marquis Warren, that little action he did there. That wasn't very honorable. I used to watch *Rawhide* when it came on, and I was impressed with the texture of the show. It seemed like the Westerns that would be akin to those done by John Ford. It had a real texture of the west.

Q: A grittiness.

A: That's the word I was looking for, yes.

Q: More authentic.

A: That's the way I thought *Gunsmoke* was, too.

Q: Those two shows, and that one Sam Peckinpah did with Brian Keith, *The Westerner*. That should have lasted longer.

A: Oh my, yes, I regret that one didn't last longer. But I also liked that *Rawhide* song by Frankie Laine. The other night I was watching one of the shows you sent me, and I thought that was such a clever touch.

Q: Any last words?

A: Well, I remember one night years ago I heard my daughter saying her prayers before she went to bed, and she said, "Please, God, don't let my daddy be the bad man all the time. Let him be the sheriff."

BIBLIOGRAPHY

BOOKS

Aylesworth, Thomas G. and John S. Bowman. *World Guide to Film Stars*. Rocky Hill, CT: NDM Publications, Inc., 1991.

Barabas, SuzAnne and Gabor Barabas. *Gunsmoke: A Complete History*. Jefferson, NC: McFarland & Co., 1990.

Brooks, Tim. *The Complete Directory to Prime Time TV Stars 1946–Present*. New York: Ballantine Books, 1987.

Brooks, Tim and Earle Marsh. *The Complete Directory to Prime Time Network and Cable TV Shows 1946–Present: 20th Anniversary Edition*. New York: Ballantine Books, 1999.

Burlingame, Jon. *TV's Biggest Hits: The Story of Television Themes From "Dragnet" To "Friends."* New York: Schirmer Books, 1996

Buscombe, Edward, ed. *The BFI Companion to the Western*. New York: Atheneum, 1988.

Cusic, Don. *Cowboys and the Wild West: An A–Z Guide from the Chisholm Trail To the Silver Screen*. New York: Facts on File, Inc., 1994.

Eliot, Marc. *American Rebel: The Life of Clint Eastwood*. New York: Harmony Books, 2009.

Forbis, William H. *The Old West: The Cowboys*. Alexandria, VA: Time-Life Books, 1977.

Garfield, Brian. *Western Films: A Complete Guide*. New York: Rawson Associates, 1982.

Green, Paul. *A History of Television's The Virginian, 1962–1971*. Jefferson, NC: McFarland & Co., 2006.

Hake, Ted. *Hake's Guide to Cowboy Character Collectibles*. Radnor, PA: Wallace-Homestead Book Company, 1994.

Maltin, Leonard. *Leonard Maltin's Classic Movie Guide*. New York: Plume, 2005.

McGilligan, Patrick. *Clint: the Life and Legend*. New York: St. Martin's Press, 2002.

Metz, Robert. *CBS: Reflections in a Bloodshot Eye*. Chicago: Playboy Press, 1975.

O'Neil, Thomas. *The Emmys*. New York: Penguin Books, 1992.

Paper, Lewis J. *Empire: William S. Paley and the Making of CBS*. New York: St. Martin's Press, 1987.

Schickel, Richard. *Clint Eastwood: A Biography*. New York: Vintage Books, 1997.

Yoggy, Gary A. *Riding the Video Range: The Rise and Fall of the Western on Television*. Jefferson, NC: McFarland & Co., 1995.

ARTICLES

"Acting Up A Stampede," *TV Guide*, Apr 18, 1959.

Cahill, Tim. Rolling Stone Interview: Clint Eastwood. *Rolling Stone*, Jul 4, 1985.

"Clint Eastwood: How To Keep Fit," *TV Guide*, Aug 15, 1959.

"Coffee Break!" *TV Guide*, Sept 2, 1961.

"Friendly Game of Pool," *TV Guide*, Sept 5, 1959.

Hano, Arnold. "How to Revive a Dead Horse or, 'Rawhide' Rides Again," *TV Guide*, Oct 2, 1965.

Jenkins, Dan. "TV Teletype," *TV Guide*, Dec 6, 1958.

Joyner, C. Courtney. "A.C. Lyles: Gentleman of the West," *Wildest Westerns*, Collectors Issue No 3, 2001

Knight, Arthur. Playboy Interview: Clint Eastwood. *Playboy*, Feb 1974.

Madden, Dennis D. "Life Line: Eric Fleming," *The TV Collector*, Nov-Dec 1990.

Magers, Boyd. "Do You Remember Rawhide?," *Western Clippings*, Nov-Dec 2003.

Magers, Boyd. "Comic Book Cowboys: Rawhide," *Western Clippings*, Sept-Oct 2008.

"Some Typical TV Longhairs," *TV Guide*, March 10, 1962.

Stahl, Bob. "TV Teletype," *TV Guide*, Apr 5, 1958.

"This Cowboy Feels He's Got It Made," *TV Guide*, Feb 4, 1961

"What I Watch: Clint Eastwood," *TV Guide*, Nov 11, 1995

Whitney, Dwight. "TV Teletype," *TV Guide*, Jun 23, 1962

INTERNET SOURCES

CITY LIVING MAGAZINE.
http://citylivingmagazine.ca/classic_actor.html

THE ERIC FLEMING HOME PAGE.
http://geocities.com/Hollywood/Hills/5176/fleming.htm

INTERNET MOVIE PRO DATABASE.
http://pro.imdb.com

LINDLEY, PHILIP. "THE RAWHIDE STORY"
http://www.book-mom.com/RAWHIDE/rawhidestory.html

INTERVIEWS OR CORRESPONDENCE (2007–2010)

RICHARD DEVON	TOM REESE
CHARLES GRAY	JAN SHEPARD
PAT HINGLE	WARREN STEVENS
L.Q. JONES	GREGORY WALCOTT
GREGG PALMER	MORGAN WOODWARD

INDEX

ABOUT THE AUTHOR

David R. Greenland has been writing professionally for more than thirty-five years. His work has appeared in numerous newspapers and magazines, including *Classic TV, Films of the Golden Age* and *Classic Images*, to which he contributes the monthly "What's Out There" column. He is the author of *Bonanza: A Viewer's Guide to the TV Legend* (recently reprinted by BearManor Media) and co-author of *Inside the Fire: My Strange Days with the Doors* by B. Douglas Cameron. He currently resides in Illinois, where he occasionally teaches creative writing at a local college.